Topz Activity Bible

Written by
Alexa Tewkesbury

CWR

Published 2015 by CWR, Waverley Abbey House, Waverley Lane, Farnham, Surrey GU9 8EP, UK.
Registered Charity No. 294387. Registered Limited Company No. 1990308.
For list of National Distributors visit www.cwr.org.uk/distributors
All Scripture references are from the Good News Bible published by The Bible Societies/Collins
© American Bible Society 1966, 1971, 1976, 1992. All rights reserved.
Concept development, editing, design and production by CWR.
Illustrated by Ben Knight at CWR.
Printed in The UK By Linney Group.
ISBN: 978-1-78259-419-2

We're called Topz because we all live at the top of something … either in houses at the top of the hill, at the top of the flats by the park, even sleeping on the top bunk counts! We are all Christians, and we go to Holly Hill School.

We love Jesus, and try to work out our faith in God in everything we do – at home, at school and with our friends. That means trying to show God's love to everyone we meet – even the Dixons Gang!

If you'd like to know more about us, visit our website **www.cwr.org.uk/topz** You can read all about us, and how you can get to know and understand the Bible more by reading our *Topz* notes, which are great fun, and written every two months just for you!

Contents

OLD TESTAMENT

NEW TESTAMENT

THE OLD TESTA

MENT

The Very Beginning

Genesis 1 and 2

In the beginning – I mean the *very* beginning, before time even began – there was no universe. No world the way we know it now. Just deep, black darkness and churning water.

You can't imagine it, can you? You just can't imagine what it must have been like when there was *nothing*.

Well, not nothing. The Creator was there. God. In the dark; across the water.

God's always been there. And God decided He wanted to make something beautiful. So He said, 'Let there be light' … and light appeared (1 v 3). God was very pleased with the brightness all around, and He separated the light from the dark. He called the light 'day' and the darkness 'night'. Then, when evening came, God smiled to Himself. It was the end of the very first day, and He'd made a good start.

On the second day, God glanced all around. 'We need something up there,' He said. 'Something to arch its way over the whole earth.' So He made the sky. The ever-changing sky! Gleaming in the daytime. Thick and black at night. Sometimes scattered with clouds, sometimes covered completely. Or my favourite – fresh and clear and blue.

Then, on the third day, God commanded, 'Let the water below the sky come together in one place, so that the land will appear' … and it was done (1 v 9). God called the land 'earth' and the water 'sea'.

But He hadn't finished yet. Day three was a busy one. 'What I'd like now,' He said, 'is for things to grow here. So let there be all sorts of plants: tall ones, short ones, leafy ones, flowery ones – even trees that will make fruit.' And, as usual, as soon as God commanded it, it happened. He gazed and nodded happily as the plants coloured in the earth. His plans were coming along very nicely.

When day number four came around, God started work again. 'Let there be lights in the sky,' He said, 'to shine down on the world that I've made.'

So He made the sun to give light through the day, and the moon to beam down through the night. He made stars, too, to glint and glisten in the night-time sky, and He thought to Himself, 'I like this, I'm very pleased.'

Well, He would be, wouldn't He? I know *I* would be!

Now, on the fifth day, God had another idea. 'There's a lot of water here,' He said. 'Let it be full of life. All kinds of fish and all sorts of water creatures. Even sea monsters!'

Sea monsters?
Like that Loch Ness one?
That's awesome!

God IS awesome! And guess what He did next: 'Let the air be filled with birds!' He said. And it was. Birds that sing, birds that squawk – birds everywhere! Then, on the sixth day, God made the animals. Wild animals, tame animals – big and small, cuddly (like my cat, Saucy) and not-so-cuddly with lots of teeth. God said, 'Let there be animals' – and there they all were. Isn't He powerful! Seriously, all He has to say is: 'Let it be!' – and it is.

After that God said, 'And now we will make human beings; they will be like us and resemble us' (1 v 26). And when God had finished, He said to the brand-new people, 'Have many children, so that your descendants will live all over the earth' (1 v 28).

At the end of the sixth day, God looked at everything he had made, and he was very pleased (1 v 31). And as everything was finished by day number seven, that's when God stopped work. He blessed the seventh day and set it apart as a special day ... And that is how the universe was created (2 v 3–4).

Here's a list of twenty amazing things that our HUGELY POWERFUL God has created. Can you find them all in the word search?

Iguana
Gazelle
Anteater
Shark
Starfish
Butterfly
Jackdaw

Hedgehog
Lioness
Antelope
Walrus
Badger
Weasel
Chameleon

Wild boar
Tortoise
Orangutan
Panda
Robin
Ostrich

Answer on p172.

```
J A C K D A W W E A S E L G
R O B I N L T O R T O I S E
T O S T R I C H O S H A R K
E S E A G L I O N E S S S R
T S W U R R I R G L W A Y R
C H A M E L E O N E I N L E
E N E A E G H N P N L T F T
A E A R D E O A O A D E R A
E L A A G I N E O L B L E E
L E B D E D N I T W O O T T
B H E G A Z E L L E A P T N
L H W A L R U S T N R E U A
I O R A N G U T A N N S B A
S T A R F I S H T A S L S L
```

12

Sarah wants to write a praise prayer to God, so she's trying to think of as many words as she can to describe God and His creation. Can you give her a head start by unscrambling the words below for her to use?

1. niecntfiMag

_____

2. oeswAme

_____

3. uautBeifl

_____

4. liaBrinlt

_____

5. Perfulow

_____

6. Mvasreoull

_____

7. gueH

_____

8. Spcceaultar

_____

9. nnStuing

_____

10. Wfnrdeuol

_____

11. Fasanttic

_____

12. eSdidnpl

_____

Answer on p172.

PRAY

Why not write your own praise prayer to God to thank Him for the wonder of His creation? Try to include as many of the words listed above as you can, and come up with some of your own, too!

In God's Garden

Genesis 2 and 3

Adam was the first man God created to live on His perfect earth. And God planted a garden in a place called Eden where Adam could live and be happy. God made sure there were plenty of fruit trees so that His new friend had food to eat. He told Adam that he could grow things in the garden, too, and take care of everything in it. (My dad would have loved that. He's crazy about anything to do with gardening!)

Then, God brought animals to Adam for him to give names to. So cool! Imagine coming up with names for all the animals! Names like hippopotamus and iguana and ostrich. I don't think I'd have called an elephant an 'elephant' though. I think I'd have called it a 'greater long-nosed flat-foot'.

But what would be a 'lesser long-nosed flat-foot'?

God and Adam were great friends. They would walk and talk together. They enjoyed each other's company. But God could see that Adam needed someone else, too. Someone to share his life and work in the garden. So God made a woman to live there with him. Her name was Eve. When God introduced her to him, Adam just couldn't stop grinning.

'At last!' he beamed. 'Here's someone just like me!'

And Adam's perfect life in the garden – that perfect place in God's perfect world – became even more so. Because that's the way God had made everything to be – perfect.

That's the way it should have stayed, too. But one day, Eve went out walking on her own.

And God had an enemy in the garden ...

Good point, Dave. Anyway, God said to Adam, 'You may eat the fruit of any tree in the garden, except the tree that gives knowledge of what is good and what is bad. You must not eat the fruit of that tree; if you do, you will die the same day' (2 v 16–17).

The snake was sneaky and shifty and sly and slippery – and any other words you can think of that mean sneaky, shifty, sly and slippery.

In a smooth, smarmy voice, the snake said to Eve, 'Did God really tell you not to eat fruit from any tree in the garden?' (3 v 1).

'Oh, no,' the woman answered. 'We can eat fruit from all the trees, except for that one right there in the middle. God said we mustn't eat the fruit from that tree. We mustn't even touch it. He said that if we do, we'll die.'

The snake slipped and slithered and gave Eve a super-sneaky smile. It hissed, 'That's not true; you will not die. God said that, because he knows that when you eat it you will be like God and know what is good and what is bad' (3 v 4–5).

Eve looked at the tree in the middle of the garden. 'That fruit does look unbelievably scrumptious,' she thought to herself. 'And … well … I do rather like the idea of becoming wise.'

'Go on,' said the snake. 'Give it a try.'

So Eve shoved God's instructions to the back of her mind, picked a fruit from the tree in the middle – and ate it. When she'd finished, she picked some for Adam, gave it to him, and he ate the fruit, too.

As soon as they had eaten it, they were given understanding (3 v 7).

Understanding is not such a bad thing, is it?

Yes! Because it wasn't just understanding about *good* things. It made Adam and Eve sad. Suddenly they knew how it felt to do something wrong. And it felt bad because they'd let God down.

What Adam and Eve did made God sad, too. Worse than sad; it broke His heart.

God still loved His friends, but what they'd done meant they couldn't share life with Him forever anymore. So He sent them away.

Out of the garden.

God did have a plan to put everything right again. But it would take a very, very long time …

Here is a list of fruits. Cross out every f, h, j and q to find out what they are, and write them out in the spaces.

1. ffPhjhiqqnjfehafjpqfjpqqlfeh

2. qqjShqtfrfjqahhwjfbqerjjqrhfyff

3. jqBhhafnhjaqna

4. fhOqrjjafqnqqghe

5. jjRhaqsffpjqbfferhqrfy

6. Afhpqrjqifchoqtj

7. qBhhlfahcjkqqchfujrrqafnht

8. ffWhjatffeqrjjmqefjlhqofnf

9. jBflqqahcjkbjjeqhrjhrfyf

10. qAqphjhpqflhef

11. hfGfojoqqsjheqbfehrrjyj

12. qPfehajqqrf

Answer on p172.

When the Rain Came Down

What a mess. When God looked at His once perfect world, that's what He saw. A mess and a muddle. The people He'd made to live there had spoilt everything. Their heads were full of bad thoughts. They were mean and selfish and unkind. God had given them a perfect place to live, and with everything they would ever need. But it wasn't enough for them.

They didn't listen to Him. They didn't live the way He wanted them to. They turned their backs on Him. All of them.

All except one man, called Noah. Noah was a good man. He still listened to God. He still loved Him and still lived the way God asked him to. And God was very pleased with him.

God said to Noah, 'I have decided to put an end to the whole human race. I will destroy them completely, because the world is full of their violent deeds' (6 v 13).

Then God told Noah to do something a bit weird. He said, 'Build a boat for yourself out of good timber; make rooms in it and cover it with tar inside and out' (6 v 14).

A boat? Erm ... why?

That's what everyone else must have asked – 'Noah, what *do* you think you're doing?' They probably had a bit of a snigger about him behind his back, too.

But Noah took no notice. God had told him to build a boat, so that's exactly what he would do. You see, out of all the people who lived on the earth, Noah and his family were the ones God had decided to save. Because only Noah was a good man.

When the boat was finished, God spoke to Noah again. 'Go inside with all your family,' He said. 'Take with you every kind of animal and bird so that we can keep them safe. And don't forget to pack up plenty of food.' God added, 'I am going to send rain that will fall for forty days and nights' (7 v 4).

No wonder He'd told Noah to build a boat!

The rain poured down – and down and down – until everything was under water. Even the very tops of mountains! But Noah trusted God to keep him, his family and all the animals safe and dry in the boat, because that's what He had promised.

After forty days, the rain stopped. **God had not forgotten Noah and all the animals with him in the boat; he caused a wind to blow, and the water started going down (8 v 1).**

Noah sent out a dove. If it came back to the boat, it would mean there was nowhere for it to land because everywhere was still under water.

The dove did come back. Noah waited for seven days, and then sent it out again. **It returned to him in the evening with a fresh olive leaf in its beak. So Noah knew that the water had gone down (8 v 11).** 'How exciting!' Noah thought. 'Won't be long now.'

When he sent the dove out for the third time, it didn't come back, and Noah knew that the earth must be all dried out. At long last.

God said to Noah, 'Go out of the boat with your wife, your sons, and their wives. Take all the birds and animals out with you, so that they may reproduce and spread over all the earth' (8 v 15–17).

As Noah stood on dry land, he gazed around, and a rainbow appeared – a ribbon of different colours that arched across the sky. 'Wow!' said Noah. It was beautiful.

God said, 'With these words I make my covenant with you: I promise that never again will all living beings be destroyed by a flood … I am putting my bow in the clouds. It will be the sign of my covenant with the world. Whenever I cover the sky with clouds and the rainbow appears, I will remember my promise' (9 v 11, 13–15).

Noah smiled. He had obeyed God because he trusted Him. And because Noah was a good, kind and obedient man, God had taken care of him.

Do you know why God was so pleased with Noah? Crack the code to find the answer in the rainbow, then write it out underneath.
a=b b=c c=d d=e e=f f=g etc

'Mnzg chc dudqxsghmf sgzs sgd KNQC bnllzmcdc.'

(Fdmdrhr 7 u 5)

'

____

____ '

____

( )

____

Answer on p172.

How much of Noah's story can you remember without looking back at it? Write down your answers!

1. What two words beginning with 'm' did God see when He looked at the world?

_____

2. What kind of a man was Noah?

_____

3. What did God tell Noah to build the boat out of?

_____

4. What did God tell Noah to make inside the boat?

_____

5. What did God tell Noah to cover the boat with, inside and out?

_____

6. How long did God send the rain for?

_____

7. What kind of bird did Noah send out to look for dry land?

_____

8. How many times did Noah send out the bird?

_____

9. When the bird brought back an olive leaf, what did that mean?

_____

10. How many times did the bird return to the boat?

_____

11. Why did God put a rainbow in the sky?

_____

12. Why did Noah do as God told him to do?

_____

Answer on p172.

God's Good Friends

Genesis 12, 17, 18 and 21

God had a good friend. A very good friend. His name was Abram.

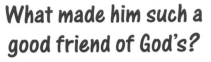

What made him such a good friend of God's?

Abram was like Noah. He listened for God's voice. He believed what God said and instructed. He obeyed because he trusted God to do what was best for him and for his wife, Sarai.

One day, God said to Abram, 'Leave your country, your relatives, and your father's home, and go to a land that I am going to show you. I will give you many descendants, and they will become a great nation.

I will bless you and make your name famous, so that you will be a blessing' (12 v 1–2).

Those were big things to ask Abram to do: move house, leave his family – *and* get ready to become a dad! Abram wasn't a young man either. He was really quite old. So it all must have seemed huge to him – especially the becoming a dad part. But Abram kept on trusting God. And because he trusted Him, he did exactly as he was told. He and Sarai packed up their bits and bobs, got together all their animals, and off they went to the new home God had chosen for them: the land of Canaan.

At long last they arrived. They knew they were in the right place, because God spoke to Abram again. He said, 'This is the country that I am going to give to your descendants' (12 v 7). Abram was so happy that God had kept them safe that he built a special altar to God right there and then – to say 'Thank You'.

But there was one thing Abram wasn't so happy about. God kept promising that he and Sarai would have descendants, but more and more time was rushing by and they still didn't have any children. And because he and Sarai were getting older and older, it got harder and harder to see how God could keep that particular promise.

God must have known what Abram was thinking. But still He promised that Abram and Sarai would have children: 'Look at the sky and try to count the stars; you will have as many descendants as that' (15 v 5). I mean – WOW – that is a LOT of descendants.

The question was – when?

Well, when Abram was ninety-nine years old – yes, *ninety-nine!* – God said, 'Your name will no longer be Abram, but Abraham, because I am making you the ancestor of many nations' (17 v 5). And then He said, 'You must no longer call your wife Sarai; from now on her name is Sarah. I will bless her, and I will give you a son by her' (17 v 15–16).

God told Abraham to call the baby boy, Isaac. But Abraham couldn't help chuckling to himself. 'I'm as good as a hundred years old,' he thought. 'And as for Sarah – she's ninety! How can we possibly have a baby now?'

After that, things started to happen.

Three men turned up outside their home one day. Abraham kindly invited them to stop for a rest and he brought them some water and some food. As the men ate, they asked, 'Where's Sarah?'

'She's indoors,' Abraham replied.

'Well,' said one of the men, 'in nine months' time, Sarah will have a baby boy.'

Sarah overheard, and it was her turn to chuckle. 'A baby? At my age? Now that would be something!'

But God said to Abraham, 'Is anything too hard for the LORD?' (18 v 14).

Well? Is it?

No! Nothing is too hard for God! Nine months later, baby Isaac was born. And Abraham and Sarah just couldn't wipe the smiles off their faces. God was smiling, too. Because He knew that one day Isaac would also have children. And Isaac's children would have children, and those children would have children – and on and on and on!

God had promised Abraham as many descendants as there are stars in the sky.

And God NEVER breaks a promise.

29

So, do you think you know Abraham and Sarah's story? Let's find out. Here's a list of words. See if you can put the right words into the right spaces below.

breaks
trusted
never
hard
best
wife

instructions
descendants
good
promise
bless

Abraham was a _____ man. He _____ God to do what was _____ for him and his _____ , Sarah, and he always followed His _____ .

God promised Abraham: 'I will _____ you and give you many _____ .'

Abraham and Sarah found God's _____ difficult to believe, but nothing is too _____ for God.

And God _____ _____ a promise.

Answer on pp172–173.

Abraham and Sarah had to pack up everything they had when God asked them to move house. When John and Sarah first moved to Holly Hill with their parents, here are some of the things that they took with them. Can you find them all in the word search?

Fridge
Books
Plates
Cooker
Sofa
Clothes
Dishwasher
Radio
Table
Curtains
Pictures
Saucepans
Toys
Toaster
Armchair
Washing machine
Computer
Lawn mower
Wardrobe
Lampshades

```
E E S C O M P U T E R O T S
W A S H I N G M A C H I N E
K C P A L S R N F T W I T S
A E S L A N R I O A A T C E
E W A A W A S Y S T B L N D
O A T I N P S R R O O E N A
R R O U M E R U O T G A P H
A D A E O C C K H D O R I S
D R S L W U S E I E S M C P
I O T B E A S R E C G C T M
O B E A R S F I I S N H U A
E E R T A C O O K E R A R L
O D I S H W A S H E R I E N
E A P L A T E S I O O R S S
```

Answer on p173.

The Wrong Son

When Isaac grew up, he married a girl called Rebecca. They had twin boys: Esau and Jacob. Even before they were born, the boys didn't get on. Rebecca could feel them inside her, fidgeting and squabbling.

Esau was born first. His skin was quite red and hairy. But Jacob's skin was as smooth as a … well … as a baby's. When Jacob was born, he was hanging on to the heel of one of Esau's teeny feet.

The boys didn't just look different. They had different personalities, too. Esau was the outdoors type. He was always on the go and he learned how to be a good hunter. But Jacob was a stay-at-home boy. He was Rebecca's favourite son, while Esau was Isaac's.

One day, when Esau came home from a hunting trip, Jacob was busy cooking some bean soup.

'Mmm! That smells good!' Esau said. 'I'm starving. Fill up a bowl for me, would you?'

Jacob stirred the soup pot thoughtfully. Then he said, 'I will give it to you if you give me your rights as the firstborn son' (25 v 31).

Hang on, that's barmy! Jacob wants Esau to give him his rights – everything Esau will get from his dad one day? Just for a bowl of soup? Never going to happen!

You think? Well, Esau got a bit dramatic and said he'd *die* if he didn't have some food right away. Jacob said, 'First make a vow that you will give me your rights' (25 v 33). Esau said, 'Fine!' – and it was all done and dusted.

What a 'souper' deal for Jacob!

As time went on, Isaac grew old and, sadly, he went blind. He knew his life would be over soon, and he wanted to give Esau, his (slightly) older son, his special blessing. So Isaac called Esau to him.

He told Esau to go out hunting, catch something, then come home and cook him up a meal. Isaac added, 'After I have eaten it, I will give you my final blessing before I die' (27 v 4). And off Esau went.

What Isaac and Esau didn't know was that Rebecca had overheard their conversation. Now, Rebecca didn't want Isaac's blessing to go to Esau. She wanted Isaac to give it to her favourite son, Jacob, instead. So she called Jacob to her.

'Jacob, listen!' she said. 'We haven't got much time. Your father is going to give Esau his special blessing today. Do exactly as I tell you to do, and you shall have it instead.'

Rebecca bustled off to cook Isaac a meal. **Then she took Esau's best clothes, which she kept in the house, and put them on Jacob. She put the skins of the goats on his arms and on the hairless part of his neck** (27 v 15–16). You see, because of his blindness, Isaac wouldn't be able to see Jacob when his younger son went to talk to him. But if he touched Jacob's skin, he would feel the goats' hair and believe he was touching Esau.

When Jacob was all ready, Rebecca gave him the food she had cooked, and he took it to Isaac.

Isaac said to Jacob, 'Please come closer so that I can touch you. Are you really Esau? … Your voice sounds like Jacob's voice, but your arms feel like Esau's arms' (27 v 21–22).

And because Jacob's skin felt hairy like Esau's, that's who Isaac thought he was. So he ate the food Jacob had brought. Then, when he had finished, he asked God to bless his son, and he made him the head of the family.

But that's rubbish! Jacob's stolen his brother's blessing. How can he get away with that?

He didn't. Not really. When Esau got back from hunting and realised how Jacob had tricked him and his father, he was hopping mad! Seriously, he was ready to kill his twin brother!

So Jacob's life was turned upside down, because that very same day, he had to leave his home and run away to live with his Uncle Laban.

Just like Esau, Benny loves soup. Here are the ingredients for his favourite chunky vegetable soup, but they are back to front. Can you write out the list the right way round?

There are also six ingredients that shouldn't be there! Put a cross beside each of the wrong ingredients.

1. noinO _____
2. otatoP _____
3. brabuhR _____
4. torraC _____
5. eeffoC _____
6. pinsraP _____
7. keeL _____
8. dratsuC _____
9. edanomeL _____
10. yelsraP _____
11. ananaB _____
12. etalocohC _____

Answer on p173.

What an extraordinary Bible story that was! Can you work out the missing words and fill in the crossword?

1. Isaac married _ _ _ _ _ _ _.

2. Jacob's brother was called _ _ _ _.

3. The two brothers were _ _ _ _ _.

4. _ _ _ _ _ was Rebecca's favourite son.

5. Esau was a good _ _ _ _ _ _.

6. When Isaac grew old, he went _ _ _ _ _.

7. Esau exchanged his rights as the firstborn son for _ _ _ _.

8. Rebecca put _ _ _ _ _ _ _ _ on Jacob's arms and neck.

Answer on p173.

Moses, God's Hero

Exodus 3 and 4

Moses was an ordinary man. That's how he thought of himself. That's what he saw if he caught sight of his reflection in a river: someone just ordinary.

Moses worked as a shepherd and he was doing just that on the day everything changed.

He was leading his father-in-law's sheep and goats across the desert and when he came to a mountain called Sinai, suddenly something caught his eye. There was a flicker; then a flame.

'That bush!' Moses gasped. 'It's on fire!'

But the fire wasn't burning the bush. Flames leapt in the air and licked at the leaves, but they weren't doing any harm at all.

Yeah! That's what Moses reckoned, too. 'This is strange,' he thought. 'Why isn't the bush burning up? I will go closer and see' (3 v 3).

But as soon as Moses took a step towards the freakily fiery bush, a voice called to him from deep inside the flames.

Freaky.

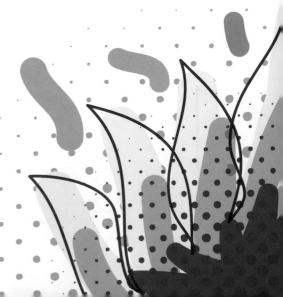

'Moses! Moses!'

Well, Moses' eyes bulged, and his jaw dropped. 'Erm … yes?' he mumbled.

The voice said, 'Do not come any closer. Take off your sandals, because you are standing on holy ground' (3 v 5). And then the voice told Moses who He was: 'I am the Lord your God!'

Well, Moses didn't know where to put himself. He was so scared, he covered his face up with his hands. He didn't dare look at the bush any longer. Not now he knew that God was in the fire.

Then God said, 'I have seen how cruelly my people are being treated in Egypt; I have heard them cry out to be rescued from their slave-drivers. I know all about their sufferings, and so I have come down to rescue them from the Egyptians and to bring them out of Egypt' (3 v 7–8).

'Jolly good,' thought Moses to himself. 'But what's any of that got to do with me?'

Then God spoke again. 'I am sending you to the king of Egypt so that you can lead my people out of his country' (3 v 10).

Moses' eyes opened wide. He dropped his hands from his face. 'But I'm just *ordinary*,' he insisted. 'Nobody special. How can I do something like that? Who would take any notice of me?'

God replied, 'I am sending you and I will be with you.'

'Right …' Moses said. 'But what happens if I tell Your people that You sent me – and they don't believe me?'

In one hand, Moses was holding a stick. 'That stick you're holding,' God said. 'Throw it on the ground.'

When Moses threw it down, it turned into a snake, and he ran away from it (4 v 3).

Eeew! Triple freaky!

It gets better! When God told Moses to pick the snake up, Moses did – and it turned back into a stick again! God said, 'Do this to prove to the Israelites that the LORD ... has appeared to you' (4 v 5).

Then God said, 'Tuck your hand inside your robe.'

So Moses did. But when he took it out again, he was horrified. It was diseased! The skin was covered in white spots.

'Tuck your hand back into your robe,' God said.

Again Moses did as he was told. This time when he brought it out, his hand was all better. 'What a relief!' he thought.

God said, 'If they will not believe you or be convinced by the first miracle, then this one will convince them' (4 v 8).

Moses shook his head. 'No, LORD, don't send me. I have never been a good speaker, and I haven't become one since you began to speak to me' (4 v 10).

But God was having none of it. 'Your brother, Aaron, can go with you,' He said. 'I will give both of you the right words. I will tell you what I want you to do.'

Moses could see there was no point arguing. God had chosen him – ordinary Moses – and He wasn't going to change His mind. So off Moses went to set God's people free and lead them out of Egypt.

Here are some statements about the story of Moses. Mark a 'T' in the box for each one you think is true, and an 'F' for each one you think is false.

Answer on p173

1. Moses was an extraordinary man.

2. Moses took care of his father-in-law's cows.

3. Moses arrived at a mountain called Sinai.

4. Moses saw a candle burning on the mountaintop.

5. God spoke to Moses through the flames.

6. God wanted Moses to make sure His people stayed in Egypt.

7. Moses was sure he was the right man for the job.

8. God turned Moses' stick into a snake.

9. God covered Moses' hand with a disease.

10. Moses thought he was a brilliant speaker.

11. God told Moses to take his mother with him to Egypt.

12. Moses obeyed God and went to Egypt.

Moses' story teaches us something very important about God and His friendship with us. Colour in every second letter of each word to find out what it is.

ACBOCD DUESFEGS
HOIRJDKILNMANROY
PPQEROSPTLUE VTWO XDYO
ZEAXBTCRDAEOFRGDHIINJAKRLY
MTNHOIPNOGRS.
SETVUEVRWYXOYNZE AIBS
CSDPEEFCGIHAIL JTKO LHMINM.

Answer on p173.

Spies in Canaan

Joshua 1 and 2

When God needed someone new to be in charge of His people, the Israelites, He chose a man called Joshua. God wanted the Israelites to have an amazing new life in the land of Canaan. And Joshua would be the man to lead them there.

What a HUGE thing to have to do for God! Joshua must have been scared. He probably didn't think he was brave enough or clever enough to do something quite so ENORMOUS.

But God said to him, 'Don't be afraid or discouraged, for I, the LORD your God, am with you wherever you go' (1 v 9). What a stonking promise! And, knowing God was right there beside him and the Israelites, Joshua started to plan how to move God's people safely into Canaan.

First, he needed to know a bit more about the place. So – and this is stonking, too! – he sent two SPIES ahead of them to go and explore. *I* could have been one of those spies! *I'd* have been an awesome spy. I still could be … Do you have to go to school if you're a spy …? Anyway, into Canaan went Joshua's spies, and when they arrived in the city of Jericho, they went to stay in the house of a woman called Rahab.

But there must have been spies spying on the spies – because the king of Jericho found out they were there. And he wasn't happy. He sent some of his men around to Rahab's house to catch them.

'Those men in your house are spies!' the king's men snarled when Rahab came to the door. 'Bring them out here now!'

Rahab stared for a moment. Then she opened her mouth to speak. Would she give them away?

'Some men did come to my house,' she answered, 'but I don't know where they were from. They left at sunset before the city gate was closed. I didn't find out where they were going, but if you start after them quickly, you can catch them' (2 v 4–6).

Wait – you didn't say anything about the spies leaving Rahab's house.

That's because they *didn't* leave. They were still there. Rahab had hidden them up on the roof of her house. She was pretty good at being a spy herself! The king's men believed every word she said and left the city to search for them.

When it was all clear, Rahab made her way up to the roof. She said to the spies, 'I know that the LORD has given you this land. Everyone in the country is terrified of you … Promise me that you will save my father and mother, my brothers and sisters, and all their families!' (2 v 9, 13).

The spies promised. Rahab had saved *them*, so they would save *her*. Rahab's house was built into the city wall. She used a long piece of rope to let the spies down to the ground through her window (so that they wouldn't be seen leaving). 'Hide in the hills for the next three days so that the king's men don't find you,' Rahab called down softly.

The men said to her, '... When we invade your land, tie this red cord to the window you let us down from. Get ... all your father's family together in your house' (2 v 17–18). You see, the red rope hanging from the window would be a sign to all the Israelites that when they marched into Jericho, the people inside Rahab's house were to be left alone.

After hiding out in the hills for three days, the spies returned to Joshua at the camp. They told him everything that had happened, and then said, 'We are sure that the LORD has given us the whole country' (2 v 23–24).

I'm sure He had, too.

Benny is pretending to be a spy. There are ten differences between these two pictures. Can you spot them all?

Answer on p173.

How much of the spy story can you remember without looking back at it? Fill in the blanks and answer the questions.

1. God said to Joshua, 'I am with you

———————— ——— ——.'

2. Where did God want His people to have a new life?

_____

3. How many spies did Joshua send?

_____

4. Where did the spies stay?

_____

5. Who heard about the spies?

_____

6. When did Rahab say that the spies left?

_____

7. Where in Rahab's house were the spies hiding?

_____

8. Rahab said to the spies, 'Everyone in the country is

———————— of you.'

9. Who does Rahab ask the spies to save?

_____

10. How did Rahab help the spies to leave her house?

_____

11. What did the spies tell Rahab to tie to her window?

_____

12. How long did the spies hide out in the hills?

_____

Answer on p173.

Gideon, the Brave and Mighty

Judges 6 and 7

God's people, the Israelites, had some enemies. They were called 'Midianites' because they came from a place called Midian. Makes sense. I suppose that makes me a 'Holly Hillite' because I come from Holly Hill.

Anyway, those Midianites were *really* nasty. They destroyed the Israelites' crops. They stole their sheep and cattle and donkeys. They left the Israelites nothing to live on. So God chose someone to help His people escape from them.

The man God picked was called Gideon. And he was a bit of a scaredy-cat. When God found him, he was hiding from the Midianites in a winepress (a sort of hole in the ground). But, rather surprisingly, God said to Gideon, 'I am with you – you *brave and mighty man*!'

HOLLY HILL

That's what God does, though. He has big stuff to do, and to help Him, He chooses the last person in the world you'd think would be able to do it.

Then the LORD ordered him, 'Go with all your great strength and rescue Israel from the Midianites. I myself am sending you' (6 v 14).

Well, Gideon obviously thought God had got this all wrong, because he replied, 'But, LORD, how can I rescue Israel? … I am the least important member of my family' (6 v 15).

God simply said, 'You can do it because I will help you' (6 v 16). And when God says something like that, you can't really argue, can you?

So Gideon blew a trumpet to call together an army. I wonder how many men he thought would join him? I bet he never dreamt there would be 32,000 of them! There were, though. An unbelievable 32,000!

Gideon was over the moon. But God is God. And God had other ideas. The LORD said to Gideon, 'The men you have are too many for me to give them victory over the Midianites. They might think that they had won by themselves, and so give me no credit. Announce to the people, "Anyone who is afraid should go back home …"' So 22,000 went back, but 10,000 stayed (7 v 2–3).

Then God told Gideon to send even more men home – until all that was left was 300 of them. Gideon must have wished he'd stayed hidden in that winepress. How was he supposed to defeat the Midianites with only 300 men?

But that night, God gave the order. 'It's time to rescue my people,' He said. 'If you're still not sure you're up to it, go to the edge of the Midianite camp and listen.'

So Gideon did. He tiptoed down. He listened – and his eyes bulged in amazement. He heard one of the men talking about a dream he'd had; he heard another man explaining what the dream meant: 'God's given Gideon victory over all of us. Over our whole army.'

Trusting God with all his heart, Gideon raced back to his camp. **He divided his 300 men into three groups and gave each man a trumpet and a jar with a torch inside it. He told them, 'When I get to the edge of the camp, watch me, and do what I do'** (7 v 16–17).

Off they crept, and at the camp edge, Gideon lifted his trumpet and blew it hard. His men copied him. Gideon threw the jar he was holding down onto the ground. It made a crash, but not nearly as big a crash as his 300 men made when they threw their jars on the ground, too. Then Gideon waved his flaming torch, and the black night was suddenly lit up bright and orange as his 300 men waved their torches in the air with him.

All together, they shouted, 'A sword for the LORD and for Gideon!' Every man stood in his place round the camp, and the whole enemy army ran away yelling (7 v 20–21). They must have thought there were thousands of Israelites after them – not just 300!

So Gideon had done it. He'd trusted God and with just 300 men, he'd seen off the whole Midianite army! God was right. His man, Gideon, really was brave and mighty.

Gideon and his men set up camp when they went to see off the Midianites. Dave was only going on holiday, but here's a list of twenty things he took with him the last time he went camping. Can you find them all in the word search?

Tent
Mug
Sleeping bag
Puzzle book
Flask
Towel
Torch
Comb
Camping stove
Sun cream
Blow up bed
Snacks
Blanket
Hat
Swimsuit
Pillow
Wellies
Folding stool
Sunglasses
Frying pan

```
B L O W U P B E D A R S T S
S L E E P I N G B A G U A S
T W W K E T O R C H R N H K
E E O S V T S S L I C N O
K L L A O E E I N A L R N O
N L L L T F S B A F I E A B
A I I F S L S M C N I A P E
L E P E G E A U K L O M G L
B S R C N L L G S R O T N Z
F O L D I N G S T O O L I Z
C O M B P O N E A W O T Y U
T E S V M I U A E C T N R P
T E N T A X S L A S T N F S
E C N C C O S W I M S U I T
```

Answer on p174.

Gideon has some exciting news for his men, but he doesn't want the Midianites to find out what it is. So he's written it in code. Can you decipher Gideon's news? Write it out under the code words.

A	C	D	E	F	G	H	I	L	M	N
1	2	3	4	5	6	7	8	9	10	11

O	P	R	S	T	U	V	W	X	Y
12	13	14	15	16	17	18	19	20	21

6 12 3   7 1 15   13 14 12 10 8 15 4 3   16 12   6 8 18 4

_____

17 15   18 8 2 16 12 14 21   12 18 4 14   12 17 14

_____

4 11 4 10 8 4 15.   3 12   4 20 1 2 16 9 21   1 15   8   3 12

_____

1 11 3   19 4   19 8 9 9   3 4 5 4 1 16   16 7 4 10.

_____

Answer on p174.

A Baby for Hannah

1 Samuel 1 and 2

Hannah was very sad. She had a good, kind husband called Elkanah. She lived quite comfortably in a little town called Ramah. But the thing Hannah wanted most in the whole wide world was a baby. A little child of her very own. And that's the one thing she didn't have.

As well as Hannah, Elkanah had another wife. Her name was Peninnah. Now Peninnah did have children – which made the fact that Hannah didn't even harder for her.

Every year, Elkanah, his two wives, Hannah and Peninnah, and Peninnah's children, made a journey to Shiloh. Lots of people travelled there to pray to God and to worship Him. It was a very special place, and every visit should have been a very special time. But for Hannah, it never was. Whenever they were there, Peninnah would tease her unkindly about having no children. She even told Hannah that it was God who had stopped her having a baby. How nasty was that? Hannah would get so upset that she couldn't eat.

Elkanah would ask, 'Hannah, why are you crying? Why won't you eat? Why are you always so sad? Don't I mean more to you than ten sons?' (1 v 8). He tried his best but he just didn't understand. And nothing he said could make Hannah feel any better.

Well, one year at Shiloh, Hannah was *so* unhappy, she couldn't stand it any longer. She took herself off and went to talk to God. She cried and cried. And in all her misery, she made God a promise.

'Almighty LORD, look at me, your servant! See my trouble and remember me! Don't forget me! If you give me a son, I promise that I will dedicate him to you for his whole life' (1 v 11).

What Hannah didn't realise was that Eli the priest was close by. He saw her talking to God. He knew she was upset. It was obvious.

When Hannah finally noticed him, she explained, 'I am desperate, and I have been praying, pouring out my troubles to the LORD' (1 v 15).

Eli nodded kindly. 'Go in peace,' Eli said, 'and may the God of Israel give you what you have asked him for' (1 v 17).

After that, Hannah felt better. Much better. She even went and had something to eat. I always feel better when I have a good heart to heart with God, too!

And then, guess what? When Elkanah, Hannah, Peninnah and Peninnah's children got home to Ramah, they'd hardly been back any time at all when Hannah realised she was expecting a baby!

A few months later, she gave birth to a little boy. She called him Samuel. God had answered her prayer and given her EXACTLY what she had asked for. At long last.

But that wasn't the end of the story. Remember Hannah's promise? If God would give her a son, she would give the boy back to Him to serve Him and work for Him. Well, after a few years, that time came.

Hannah took Samuel to Shiloh. She found Eli the priest and said, 'I am the woman you saw standing here, praying to the LORD. I asked him for this child, and he gave me what I asked for. So I am dedicating him to the LORD' (1 v 26–28).

Then Hannah went home to Ramah, leaving Samuel with Eli to serve God at Shiloh. She visited him once a year, but it must have been very hard for her to leave him behind. Still, it's the promise she'd made to God, and a promise she had to keep.

And because Hannah kept her promise, God had a surprise for her. Well – five surprises actually. Three more sons and two daughters! Brothers and sisters for Samuel, and a wonderful new family.

Ha! I love that story!

Here are some statements about Hannah's story. Mark a 'T' in the box for each one you think is true, and an 'F' for each one you think is false.

1. Hannah wanted a baby more than anything.

2. Hannah's husband was called Eli.

3. Hannah had a sister called Peninnah.

4. Peninnah had children of her own.

5. Every year, Hannah and her husband went to a special place called Ramah to worship God.

6. Hannah was so unhappy that she lost her appetite.

7. Hannah promised God that if He gave her a son, she would give him back to God.

8. When Hannah prayed to God and asked Him for a baby, her husband overheard her.

9. After she had finished praying, Hannah was still unhappy.

10. God answered Hannah's prayer and she had a baby boy.

11. Hannah called her baby Elkanah.

12. Hannah broke her promise to God.

Answer on p.174

Josie's auntie has just had a baby boy and Josie and her family want to buy him a present. Here are the Topz Gang's present suggestions, but they're back to front. Use the spaces to write them out the right way round and find out what they are!

1. elttaR _____

2. erutciP koob _____

3. seitooB _____

4. taH _____

5. yddeT _____

6. yldduC ynnub _____

7. toC elibom _____

8. teknalB _____

9. gnignahC tam _____

10. ybaB htab _____

11. thgiN thgil _____

12. rebbuR kcud _____

Answer on p174.

A New King

The country of Israel needed a king. So God chose a man called Saul to do the job. But things didn't go very well. They started out all right, but then Saul stopped listening to God. And when he stopped listening, he stopped doing the things God wanted him to do – and started doing things God didn't want him to do at all. God was disappointed, and sorry that he had made Saul king of Israel (15 v 35). So, He decided to make someone else king of Israel instead.

There was a man called Samuel who had grown up serving God. He and God were good friends. God knew that Samuel was sad about Saul, but He wanted Samuel to do something for Him.

The LORD said to Samuel, 'How long will you go on grieving over Saul? I have rejected him as king of Israel. But now get some olive oil and go to Bethlehem, to a man named Jesse, because I have chosen one of his sons to be king' (16 v 1).

Samuel's eyes went wide. His stomach knotted up and he felt really scared. Why did God want him to do this? It sounded like quite a bad idea.

'Erm …' he murmured. 'The thing is …' he mumbled. 'It's just … well … how can I do that? What happens if Saul hears about it? I'll tell you what'll happen – he'll kill me, that's what!'

But God had a plan and nothing was going to get in the way. Not even Samuel's fear.

Which is good, because God's plans are always for the best, even if we can't see it at the time.

Oh, yes, the very, very best. God said, 'You will anoint as king the man I tell you to' (16 v 3). So all Samuel could do was gulp, suck in a deep breath, and set off on the road for Bethlehem.

Soon after Samuel arrived, he found Jesse, and Jesse introduced him to the first of his sons.

'This is Eliab,' Jesse said.

Well, when Samuel saw Eliab, he was sure this must be the man God wanted to be the new king of Israel.

But the LORD said to him, 'Pay no attention to how tall and handsome he is. I have rejected him, because I do not judge as people judge. They look at the outward appearance, but I look at the heart' (16 v 7).

Next, Jesse introduced Samuel to his son, Abinadab. But when Abinadab stood in front of Samuel, God said nothing at all. So Samuel said, 'No, the LORD hasn't chosen him either' (16 v 8).

'Shammah!' Jesse called. And another one of Jesse's sons came to meet Samuel. But again, Samuel didn't hear God's voice so he shook his head and said, 'No, it's not you.'

In this way Jesse brought seven of his sons to Samuel. And Samuel said to him, 'No, the LORD hasn't chosen any of these.' Then he asked him, 'Have you any more sons?' (16 v 10–11).

What we look like isn't what's important to God. He cares about what's inside. The sort of people we are. Don't you just love that?

'Well,' said Jesse, 'there's my youngest. But he's out in the fields looking after the sheep.'

'Then ask him to come and see me,' said Samuel. So Jesse sent for him. He was a handsome, healthy young man, and his eyes sparkled. The LORD said to Samuel, 'This is the one ... anoint him!' (16 v 12).

The boy's name was David. Samuel took the olive oil he'd brought with him, and, as the other seven brothers watched, he poured some onto David's head. This was a sign that David had been chosen by God. And straightaway, God's Holy Spirit came to live inside him.

David smiled. One day, he would be Israel's new king, and he knew God would be with him all the way.

King Saul disobeyed God, so God decided that he wouldn't be king of Israel anymore – and nothing would change His mind. Cross out every v, x, and z to find out what God said to Samuel.

'I xamz vsxoxrrzy xtxhzzatv Iv
mxvazdxev Sxvazzuxl zkzixnvgx;
xhvezx hvxaxsvz vtzzuxzrvnxvezdz
avxwxzavy zfxrvoxxmz vmxezv
xanvdz dixszovxbzeyvvexdz mzy
xcvomzvmvzaxnzdvs.'

(1 Samuel 15 v 11)

Now cross out every p, q and z to find out what Samuel said to Saul.

'Tqqhzep LppOzRqD pzhqqazsz
ztpqozrznq tpzhqqez
pkqizznqpgpdzzoqmq qoqfq
lppszqrppazeqlq zapwqaqyz qqfprzozmq
pyqqozuq ztzozdpqayq ... Gzopd
pdqozezspz qznoptp lqizep ppzoqr
qcpphzqapngzez zhpiqsz pqmziqznpd.'

(1 Samuel 15 v 28–29)

Answer on p174.

God has chosen the next king of Israel! Can you help Samuel get to the right son?

Answer on p174.

67

Solomon, the Wise

1 Kings 2 and 3

I'm glad my name's Dave. That makes me a tiny bit – just a very, very teeny tiny bit – like King Dave: David, the boy who looked after sheep and was chosen by God to be the king of Israel.

David was an awesome king. He reigned for forty years with God right beside him. Then, when he grew old, he passed his crown on to his son, Solomon, and gave him these instructions: 'Be confident and determined, and do what the LORD your God orders you to do. Obey all his laws and commands … so that wherever you go you may prosper in everything you do' (2 v 2–3).

Solomon loved his father, and he loved God, too. So, when King David died and Solomon at last took over, he was very careful to follow the instructions his dad had given him.

God was pleased with the new King Solomon, and to show him just how happy He was, God decided to give Solomon a present.

That night the LORD appeared to him in a dream and asked him, 'What would you like me to give you?' (3 v 5).

Woah! Seriously? God *seriously* asked King Solomon what present he'd like? He could ask for anything! All the money in the whole world!

Yup, King Solomon could have asked for anything. After all, God is God and He can do and give anything He wants.

But, do you know what? King Solomon didn't ask for just *anything*. He didn't ask for money, or power, or loads of servants, or to live a massively long life in the poshest palace in the whole history of posh palaces.

Nope.

Then what *did* he ask for?

King Solomon said to God, 'O LORD God, you have let me succeed my father as king, even though I am very young and don't know how to rule ... So give me the wisdom I need to rule your people with justice and to know the difference between good and evil. Otherwise, how would I ever be able to rule this great people of yours?' (3 v 7, 9).

Well, God was pleased. Really pleased. Solomon hadn't asked to be rich, or to live in a posh palace. He hadn't even asked for a super-long life. What Solomon had asked for was something totally unselfish. Something that would help him serve God and be the best king he could possibly be to God's people.

Woah again! So Solomon could have asked God for anything in the whole world, but he asked for *wisdom*. That's really very ... wise ... isn't it?

So God smiled and said, 'I will do what you have asked. I will give you more wisdom and understanding than anyone has ever had before or will ever have again (3 v 12).

And then, just to show exactly how happy Solomon had made Him, God added, 'I will also give you what you have not asked for: all your life you will have wealth and honour, more than that of any other king. And if you obey me and keep my laws and commands, as your father David did, I will give you a long life' (3 v 13–14).

That's right! God gave him all the other stuff anyway!

When King Solomon woke up from his sleep he knew that, yes, he was dreaming, but what God had promised was not a dream! God *really* had spoken to him and was *really* going to give him some amazing presents. So he jumped out of bed straightaway, and hurried off out to thank God and to praise Him.

Solomon was quite the clever clogs. Do you reckon you're a wise one, too? Well then, work out the missing words and fill in the crossword!

1. _ _ _ _ _ was king before Solomon.

2. Solomon's dad reigned for _ _ _ _ _ years.

3. God was _ _ _ _ _ _ _ with the new king.

4. God wanted to give Solomon a _ _ _ _ _ _ _.

5. God spoke to Solomon in a _ _ _ _ _.

6. Solomon asked for wisdom to rule with _ _ _ _ _ _ _.

7. Solomon didn't ask for money but God said He would give him _ _ _ _ _ _.

8. God also promised Solomon a _ _ _ _ life.

Answer on p174.

When it was the Topz Gang's birthdays, they weren't promised presents in a dream, but they did each get something they really wanted. Can you guess whose present is whose? Draw a line to link the right Gang member with the right present.

Answer on p174.

Nehemiah Builds a New City

The city of Jerusalem was destroyed. There had been a war and now it was just rubble and ruins. God's people would never be able to live there or worship God there again, unless it could be rebuilt.

But who could take on such a massive job?

A man called Nehemiah was very sad when he heard that Jerusalem's walls were still all broken, and that the city gates were left black and charred where they had been burnt. Jerusalem was where his ancestors had once lived, and he wanted God's people to be able to go back and live there safely again.

'If only I could travel to Jerusalem,' Nehemiah thought. 'If only I could see the damage for myself and start to rebuild the city.'

But he wasn't free just to get up and go. Nehemiah had a job. He worked as a wine steward for the emperor of Persia, whose name was Artaxerxes.

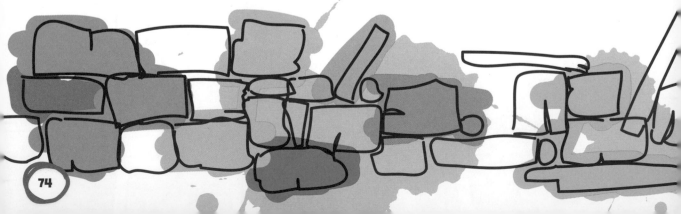

That's quite a name! Just so you know, it's pronounced 'Art-ack-zerk-seas'. Give it a go!

Now, Nehemiah knew that the only way he'd be able to get some time off to go to Jerusalem and start building it again was if God helped him. So he prayed. And he prayed *hard*. He didn't even eat for a few days just to show God how serious he was in his prayers.

About four months later, Nehemiah was serving the emperor with his wine, when he noticed the emperor peering at him. Then the emperor asked, 'Why are you looking so sad? You aren't ill, so it must be that you're unhappy' (2 v 2).

Nehemiah was taken by surprise. He didn't think the emperor would notice something like that, but he couldn't let the chance slip by.

So he said, 'How can I help looking sad when the city where my ancestors are buried is in ruins and its gates have been destroyed by fire?' (2 v 3).

Well, Nehemiah was even more surprised when Emperor Artaxerxes asked, 'So what do you want?'

Nehemiah quickly asked God to help him find the right words to speak to the emperor. Then he said, 'If Your Majesty is pleased with me and is willing to grant my request, let me go to the land of Judah, to the city where my ancestors are buried, so that I can rebuild the city' (2 v 5).

Nehemiah waited. How was this going to go?

Well, I can tell you that if Nehemiah had been sitting down, he would have fallen off his chair! Because what the emperor said was, 'Yes, you may go!' Just like that!

And when Nehemiah asked the emperor for some wood from his forests so that there would be plenty for all the new building, the emperor said, 'Yes, take all that you need!' Emperor Artaxerxes even sent some of his soldiers to travel with Nehemiah to keep him safe!

So Nehemiah knew God had heard his prayers. Nehemiah knew God was with him. And off he went to Jerusalem.

When he got there, Nehemiah waited for three days before he told anyone about his plans. Then, in the middle of the night, he took a few people with him, and rode on a donkey all around the city. He had a good look at all the ruins and saw exactly what needed to be done. And he told everyone how God was with him and would help him – how God would help all of them. And the people said, 'Let's start rebuilding!' And they got ready to start the work (2 v 18).

When God's enemies heard about Nehemiah's plans, they laughed at them. They didn't believe for one minute that Nehemiah could rebuild a city.

But Nehemiah knew differently. He said, 'The God of Heaven will give us success. We are his servants, and we are going to start building' (2 v 20).

God did give them success, too. Stone by stone He was with them and He helped them. Until the new city of Jerusalem was finished.

Nehemiah has been busy rebuilding Jerusalem. Here are two houses that he and his friends have put back together. They look very similar, but can you spot the ten differences between them?

Answer on p175.

Can you crack the code to discover a very important question and answer at the heart of Nehemiah's rebuilding story?

a=b   b=c   c=d   d=e   e=f   f=g etc

Vgx chc Mdgdlhzg'r okzmr rtbbddc?

Adbztrd gd sqtrsdc Fnc dudqx rsdo ne sgd vzx.

Answer on p175.

The Man God Chose
Jeremiah 1 and 38

Jeremiah was special, but he didn't know it. Until God said to him one day, 'I chose you before I gave you life, and before you were born I selected you to be a prophet to the nations' (1 v 5).

Erm ... sorry ... a what to the what?

A prophet to the nations. In other words, God had chosen Jeremiah before he was born – before he was a flicker of life in his mum's tummy even – to tell people what He wanted to say to them.

Jeremiah heard God speak. He glanced over one shoulder. And then the other. There was no one else around. But surely God couldn't be talking to *him* ... could He?

'The thing is, God,' Jeremiah gulped, 'I don't know how to talk to people. And I'm not even very old. In fact I'm really young.'

God replied, 'Do not say that you are too young, but go to the people I send you to, and tell them everything I command you to say. Do not be afraid of them, for I will be with you to protect you' (1 v 7–8).

Then God stretched out His hand, and guess what He did? He actually touched Jeremiah's lips! God said, 'Listen, I am giving you the words you must speak' (1 v 9).

But even so, being God's messenger wouldn't be easy. God's people wouldn't want to hear what God had to say. They'd turned their backs on Him. They didn't care what He thought. They didn't even listen to Him anymore. God had done nothing but good things for them, and they behaved as if He wasn't there.

It would be Jeremiah's job to tell them that God had been very patient with them, but now He wanted them to turn back to Him. And Jeremiah would have to warn them that if they didn't, then bad things would happen.

The message Jeremiah was spreading eventually reached the ears of some important men. Some powerful men. As soon as they heard what he was saying, they stormed off to see the king.

'You can't let Jeremiah get away with saying these things,' they grumbled. 'We must get rid of him. Our soldiers are starting to get nervous! So is everyone else. Jeremiah's not trying to help us. He wants to hurt us.'

The king shook his head. He didn't know what to do. He just said, 'Very well, then, do what you wish with him; I can't stop you' (38 v 5).

So the important and powerful men found Jeremiah and grabbed hold of him. They tied ropes around him and they lowered him down into a deep, dark well. Then they left him there! There was no water in the well, just thick, oozy, black mud. Jeremiah sank down into it. He was cold and filthy and uncomfortable.

· And all alone.

At least, the important and powerful men *thought* he was all alone. But Jeremiah knew he wasn't. God was with Him and would take care of him – because that's what He had promised. Remember? 'Do not be afraid ... for I will be with you to protect you' (1 v 8).

A servant called Ebedmelech worked at the royal palace. When he heard what the men had done to Jeremiah, he scurried off to see the king.

He said, 'Your Majesty, what these men have done is wrong. They have put Jeremiah in the well, where he is sure to die of starvation' (38 v 9).

The king listened to Ebedmelech. He ordered him to take three men with him to the well to rescue Jeremiah. Ebedmelech did as he was told. Then, with some long ropes and with the help of the three men, he pulled Jeremiah up and out of the mud. Up into the daylight.

You see? God had chosen Jeremiah to speak for Him, and just as He had promised, God had looked after him.

Here are some statements about the story of Jeremiah. Mark a 'T' in the box for each one you think is true, and an 'F' for each one you think is false.

1. God knew Jeremiah before he was born.

2. Jeremiah thought he was too old to speak for God.

3. God touched Jeremiah's ears.

4. God's people didn't want to hear what God had to say.

5. God didn't care whether His people turned back to Him or not.

6. Some important men wanted to get rid of Jeremiah.

7. Jeremiah was lowered down into a well.

8. The well was full of water.

9. The king's name was Ebedmelech.

10. The king ordered Jeremiah to be rescued.

11. The king's servant pulled Jeremiah out of the well all by himself.

12. God took care of Jeremiah, just as He promised He would.

Answer on p175

Look at these two lists of words. The first list describes the sort of people God wants us to be. The second list describes the sort of people God *doesn't* want us to be. Draw a line to link each word in the first list with the word that means the opposite in the second list. Then see if you can find all the words in the word search!

Kind	Naughty
Gentle	Proud
Humble	Selfish
Generous	Difficult
Loving	Rude
Respectful	Mean
Giving	Hateful
Obedient	Nasty
Joyful	Grumpy
Helpful	Harsh

```
N G L O V I N G P R O U D
A E Y E A A H E L P F U L S
U N P E E H H N A S T Y L L
G E M M A U R S U U T N L L
H R U H A R S H I R T N L F
T O R E S P E C T F U L F F
Y U G P A A R S N O L D V E
L S E E H A T E F U L E E E
H U M B L E R I O T U R S S
A H O B E D I E N T I H S O
U E D I F F I C U L T S O D
E J O Y F U L I O K I N D
G E N T L E I G I V I N G
```

Answer on p175.

85

THE NEW TESTA

MENT

The Baby in the Stable

The very first Christmas started with an angel. Well, sort of. Because God sent an angel called Gabriel to Nazareth, to visit a girl called Mary. God had a message for her.

When Mary saw an angel appear right in front of her, she was terrified out of her wits! But the angel Gabriel said, 'Don't be afraid, Mary; God has been gracious to you. You will become pregnant and give birth to a son, and you will name him Jesus. He will be great and will be called the Son of the Most High God' (Luke 1 v 30–32).

Mary was confused. 'Are you saying,' she murmured, 'that God is sending His Son to the earth as a baby – and He wants *me* to be the baby's mother? How can I do that? I haven't even got a husband yet!'

But God had already thought of this. He sent an angel to speak to a man called Joseph, too. The angel gave Joseph God's message in a dream: 'Marry Mary,' the angel said. 'It's what God wants you to do. Then you can bring up God's Son together.'

So when Joseph woke up, he married Mary, as the angel of the Lord had told him to do (Matthew 1 v 24).

The months went by and at last it was nearly time for the baby Jesus to be born. But instead of Mary being able to have a bit of a rest (because babies can be hard work – that's what my mum says anyway), Mary and Joseph had to go on a journey. The emperor wanted to know how many people there were, so everyone travelled to their home town to be counted.

Mary and Joseph had to go to Bethlehem, and Mary was worn out when they got there. Still, *now* maybe she could have her rest. But the town was so busy with all the other people who had come to be counted, that there was nowhere for them to stay. And Mary could tell the baby was on His way. What were they going to do?

It was an innkeeper who saved the day. He didn't have a spare room in his inn, but he did have a stable where Mary could lie down.

As it turned out, it was in the stable where Jesus was born. In amongst the bales of hay and the curious animals. And Mary tucked Him up in a feeding trough.

Hard to believe that God's Son – His very own Son! – wasn't born in a palace or a castle. Just a dirty, dingy stable.

Hard to believe that Jesus' first visitors weren't kings and queens and lords and ladies either. But they weren't. The first people God chose to tell about the birth of Jesus were some shepherds. They were out in the hills looking after their sheep.

An angel of the Lord appeared to them, and the glory of the Lord shone over them (Luke 2 v 9). They were SO scared – just like Mary was when an angel appeared to her!

But the angel said, 'Don't be afraid! I am here with good news for you, which will bring great joy to all the people. This very day ... your Saviour was born ... Christ the Lord! And this is what will prove it to you: you will find a baby wrapped in strips of cloth and lying in a manger' (Luke 2 v 10–12).

Then the sky was lit up with a whole army of angels, all singing their hearts out to God.

Well, the shepherds didn't waste any time. They said to each other, 'Let's go to Bethlehem and see this thing that has happened, which the Lord has told us' (Luke 2 v 15). And off they trotted. Jesus' very first visitors.

Later Jesus had some other visitors, too. They were wise men who studied the stars. When they spotted a new star in the sky, they realised that someone very special had been born. So they followed the star and it led them right to Jesus. They gave Him presents: gold and frankincense and myrrh. And they got down on their knees and they worshipped Him.

Look very closely at these ten shepherds. They may all look exactly the same, but one of them isn't. Can you spot the odd one out?

Answer on p176.

Colour in the dotted shapes to discover the words the angels sang in the skies near Bethlehem.

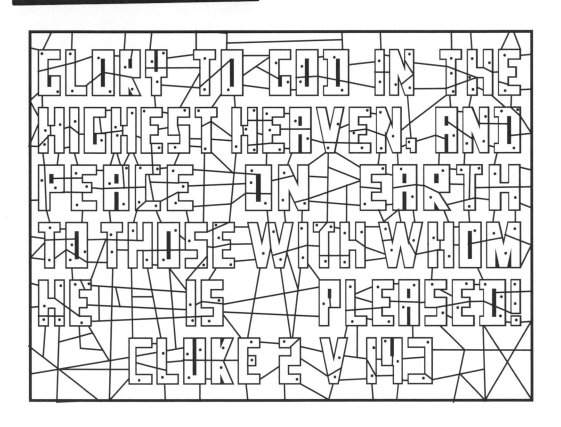

Answer on p176

Now decorate the rest of the page with Christmassy patterns to make it really festive!

The Boy Who Wasn't Lost

Luke 2

Mary and Joseph were on their way home to Nazareth. They'd been to Jerusalem – a big city – to celebrate the Passover festival with their twelve-year-old boy, Jesus. God's people, crowds and crowds of them, joined in with the festival every year to remember how much God loved them and to thank Him for all the good things He had done for them. So, as Mary and Joseph walked along the road that took them away from the city and the finished festival, there were lots of other people with them.

They thought Jesus was with them, too. They weren't sure exactly where, but He'd be certain to be with some of the other children in the group. Or tagging along with some of the grown ups. He was definitely there, of course He was … Where else would He be …?

After Mary and Joseph had been walking for a day, Mary asked Joseph, 'Have you seen Jesus?'

'No, why? Haven't you?' Joseph asked Mary.

They started asking the people around them – 'I don't suppose you've seen Jesus, have you?' They turned around and made their way through the groups and huddles walking along the road with them. 'Have you seen Jesus?' they asked. 'Has *anyone* seen Jesus?'

But no one had.

Mary started to panic. Well, you would, wouldn't you? I know *my* mum would if she lost *me*. Joseph's eyes flicked from group to group and face to face. 'Where are You, Jesus?' he muttered to himself. 'Where *are You*?'

There was no sign. Just no sign of Him anywhere.

So, what else could Mary and Joseph do? They had to go back to Jerusalem. If no one had seen Jesus, He must still be in the city. He must have got left behind.

They hurried as much as they could. But it had taken them a good day to get this far towards their home in Nazareth, so it would take another day to get back to Jerusalem.

When they arrived, they searched and they searched. Down wide streets, up narrow streets, in amongst market stalls. Until at long last – at ultra-long last – they found him in the Temple, sitting with the Jewish teachers, listening to them and asking questions. All who heard him were amazed at his intelligent answers (2 v 46–47).

Mary and Joseph couldn't believe their eyes. They didn't know whether to be cross with Him for disappearing on them, or thrilled to bits because He was safe!

Jesus looked quite calm. Quite happy. Mary couldn't understand it. Jesus was such a good boy. How could He do something so thoughtless? Disappear without telling them where He was?

She said, 'My son, why have you done this to us? Your father and I have been terribly worried trying to find you' (2 v 48).

Now it was Jesus' turn not to understand. He looked puzzled and said, 'Why did you have to look for me? Didn't you know that I had to be in my Father's house?' (2 v 49).

Of course! Makes perfect sense. Jesus really did think Mary and Joseph would know where He was. After all, He's God's Son, so the Temple – His Father's house – is where He'd feel most at home.

I suppose it was quite hard for Mary and Joseph to understand that. But Jesus was a good boy. While He was growing up, He had two parents on earth. They loved Him and would look after Him, and He knew it was important to love and respect them, too, and obey them.

So Jesus left the Temple and went home with them to Nazareth, where He grew up to be strong and healthy and very wise. Everyone liked Him. And His Father in heaven looked down on Him day after day – and smiled.

When the time came for Jesus to leave His home and start to tell people about God and His love and forgiveness, God knew His Son would have grown into a brilliant Teacher.

Can you help Mary and Joseph find their way through the maze to where Jesus is talking in the Temple?

Answer on p176.

So, Mary and Joseph did find Jesus in the end. Phew! Can you work out the missing words and fill in the crossword?

1. Mary and Joseph were travelling home from _ _ _ _ _ _ _ _ _.

2. God's people had been celebrating the festival called _ _ _ _ _ _ _ _.

3. When Mary and Joseph realised Jesus wasn't with them, they were very _ _ _ _ _ _ _.

4. Mary and Joseph _ _ _ _ _ _ _ _ for Jesus.

5. Jesus was finally found in the _ _ _ _ _ _.

6. Jesus was talking to the _ _ _ _ _ _ _ _.

7. People were _ _ _ _ _ _ at how much Jesus knew and understood.

8. Jesus called the Temple, 'My _ _ _ _ _ _'s house'.

Answer on p176.

The First Followers

Jesus stood by the lake. He could see people coming towards Him – a big crowd of people. It was growing bigger all the time. Jesus knew these people had heard about Him. They wanted Him to teach them about God. He wanted to teach them, too, but there were so many of them. If He stayed where He was, they'd push and shove and it would be impossible to talk to them. What He needed was a plan.

That's when He spotted the two boats. They were pulled up onto the beach and the fishermen they belonged to were busy washing their nets.

Jesus jumped into the boat belonging to Simon Peter and his brother, Andrew (Matthew 4 v 18).

'Push me out onto the water a little, would you, please?' Jesus said.

The brothers did as He asked. And from out on the lake, Jesus taught all the people on the shore as He sat in the fishing boat, bobbing gently up and down.

When he had finished speaking, he said to Simon, 'Push the boat out further to the deep water, and you and your partners let down your nets for a catch' (Luke 5 v 4).

Simon Peter sighed and looked at his brother, Andrew. Andrew glanced back at him and shrugged his shoulders. It was obvious that neither of them wanted to fish anymore today. They'd tried already – they'd stuck at it all through the night – and they hadn't caught a thing.

Simon Peter glanced back towards Jesus. 'Master,' Simon answered, 'we worked hard all night long and caught nothing. But if you say so, I will let down the nets' (Luke 5 v 5).

So that's what the two fishermen did. They sailed out further and dropped the nets down into the water because Jesus had told them to. But they couldn't help shaking their heads as if to say, 'What a waste of time.'

Haha! They didn't know who Jesus was, did they?

No, they didn't. But they were about to find out!

It happened almost the second the nets hit the water. Suddenly, the lake around the boat was alive with fish! Teeming, bubbling, *frothing*!

'Look at that!' cried Simon Peter. 'Would you just look at that!'

He and his brother started to haul up the nets, only to find that they were so full of fish, they could hardly drag them back into the boat.

Simon Peter signalled to the two fishermen who owned the other boat Jesus had seen on the beach. 'James! John! Come and help! Come and help us!' he yelled.

They came and filled both boats so full of fish that the boats were about to sink (Luke 5 v 7). The nets were so heavy with the catch that it took every bit of the fishermen's strength to heave and haul and drag them back on board.

And at that moment, as the fishermen puffed and gasped and stared at the huge number of fish on the decks, all at once, they realised who Jesus was.

Catching *people*?
What does that
mean?

They understood that He must have been sent by God. He'd done something unbelievable – something *impossible* – right in front of their very eyes.

When Simon Peter saw what had happened, he fell on his knees before Jesus and said, 'Go away from me, Lord! I am a sinful man!' (Luke 5 v 8). He didn't think he was good enough to be anywhere near someone as important and special as Jesus.

But Jesus smiled and said, 'Don't be afraid; from now on you will be catching people' (Luke 5 v 10).

Jesus wanted the fishermen to join Him in 'catching people for God' – teaching them about God and about how to be God's friends.

And those four ordinary fishermen – Simon Peter, Andrew, James and John – they didn't even stop to have a think about it. **They pulled the boats up on the beach, left everything, and followed Jesus** (Luke 5 v 11).

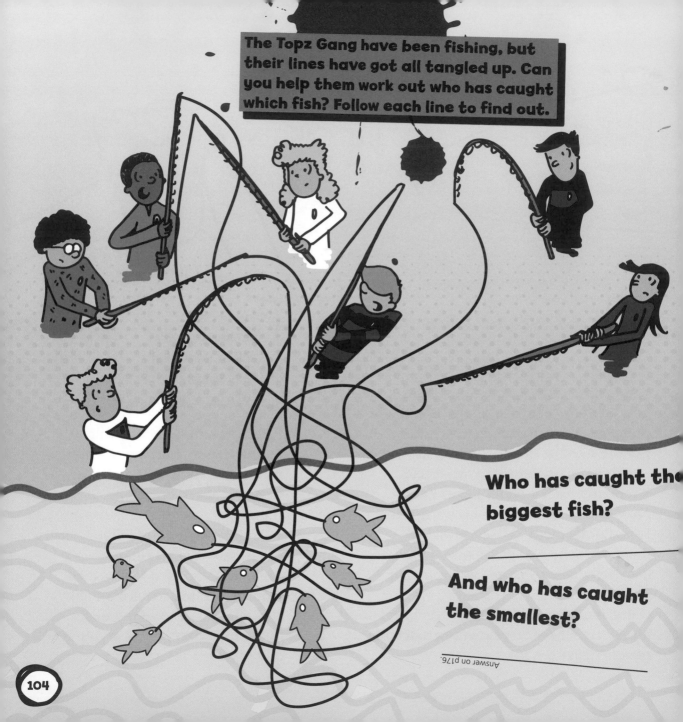

The Topz Gang have been fishing, but their lines have got all tangled up. Can you help them work out who has caught which fish? Follow each line to find out.

Who has caught the biggest fish?

And who has caught the smallest?

Answer on p176.

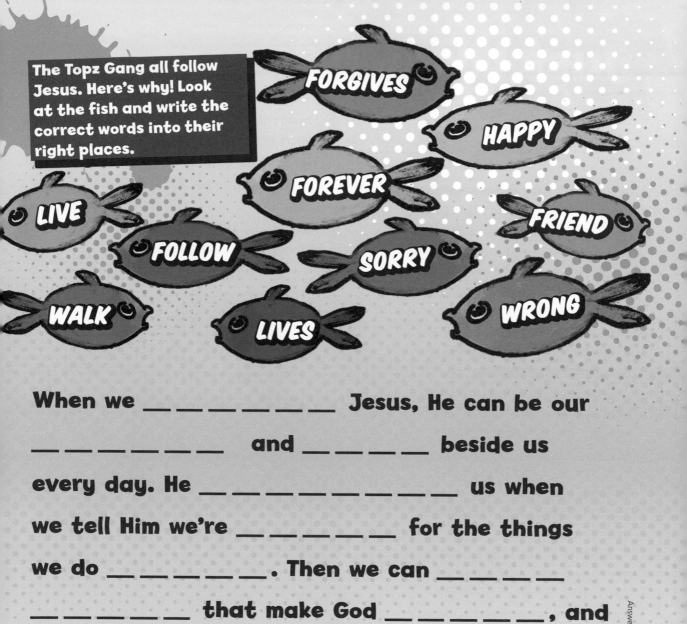

The Topz Gang all follow Jesus. Here's why! Look at the fish and write the correct words into their right places.

FORGIVES

HAPPY

FOREVER

LIVE

FRIEND

FOLLOW

SORRY

WALK

LIVES

WRONG

When we _ _ _ _ _ _ _ Jesus, He can be our

_ _ _ _ _ _ _ and _ _ _ _ beside us

every day. He _ _ _ _ _ _ _ _ _ us when

we tell Him we're _ _ _ _ _ for the things

we do _ _ _ _ _. Then we can _ _ _ _

_ _ _ _ _ that make God _ _ _ _ _ _, and

one day we will be with Him _ _ _ _ _ _ _.

Answer on p176.

Just Like Mary

Luke 10

Jesus had been working very hard. He'd been travelling from place to place with His special friends, the disciples. He'd been teaching all about God and how to have a life with Him forever. He'd been healing people who were sick, too. Talking to them, making them better. Working miracles! Jesus had time for everyone.

One day, he came to a village where a woman named Martha welcomed him in her home (10 v 38).

'Come in, Jesus, come in!' Martha beamed. 'It's not much, but it's home, and You're very welcome in it.'

Martha shared the house with her sister, Mary. When Mary saw Jesus step through the front door, her eyes opened wide with amazement, and her jaw dropped.

I'm not surprised. If Jesus suddenly turned up at *my* house, I think my jaw would drop right off! And as for my mum, she wouldn't know where to put herself. She'd probably ask Jesus to try out all the chairs in the lounge and then pick the one He found the most comfy. And even then, she'd never stop fussing with the cushions!

I know, Paul! Mine, too! Can you imagine it?

Well, anyway, Mary and Martha had been busy doing housework: washing, sweeping, cleaning, baking bread and so on. But the minute Mary realised Jesus was stopping for a visit, she downed tools.

She took off her apron, dusted herself down, and said, 'Do come and sit here, Lord.'

Then Mary sat down, too, **at the feet of the Lord and listened to his teaching** (10 v 39).

And she forgot everything else. All the chores, the only-half-done baking. All Mary wanted was to be close to Jesus for the little time that He was in her house, and to listen to everything He had to say and teach.

In fact, Mary was SO wrapped up in listening to Jesus, she didn't realise that Martha wasn't sitting and listening, too. You see, even though she'd invited Jesus into the house to spend some time with them, Martha was still busying herself with all the housework. And the fact that Mary now wasn't lifting a finger to help her was *not* going down too well.

Uh oh! That's like my mum, too. If I'm supposed to be helping out with the hoovering or something and I get distracted – which I often do because, let's face it, there are just so many more interesting things to do than hoovering – she really gets quite grumpy. I mean, I still might get a slice of cake when I get in from school, but it probably won't be chocolate.

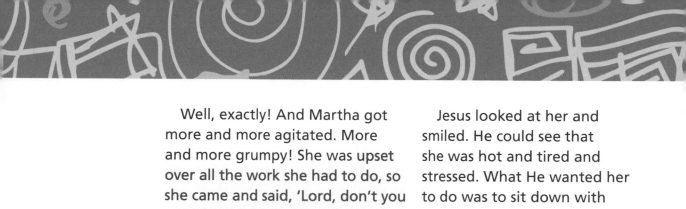

Well, exactly! And Martha got more and more agitated. More and more grumpy! She was upset over all the work she had to do, so she came and said, 'Lord, don't you care that my sister has left me to do all the work by myself? Tell her to come and help me!' (10 v 40).

I think she was even a bit cross with Jesus!

Jesus looked at her and smiled. He could see that she was hot and tired and stressed. What He wanted her to do was to sit down with Mary, to rest and to listen.

Jesus said, 'Martha, Martha! You are worried and troubled over so many things, but just one thing is needed. Mary has chosen the right thing, and it will not be taken away from her' (10 v 41–42).

There's always stuff: stuff to do, stuff to plan, stuff to think about. But sometimes, what we really need to do is just sit down and be with Jesus. Just like Mary.

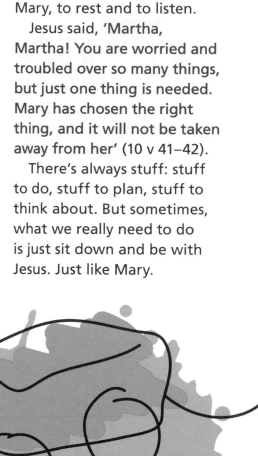

Here are twenty items that are all to do with cleaning the house and tidying the garden. Can you find them in the word search?

Fork
Spade
Rake
Hoe
Cloth
Polish
Broom

Bleach
Duster
Scourer
Lawn mower
Hedge cutter
Shears
Watering can

Sink unblocker
Washing up liquid
Vacuum cleaner
Washing powder
Rubber gloves
Dustpan and brush

```
D W H S U R C S C O U R E R W H
R O A K C I A B H D O O U Q A S
E D U S T P A N A N D B R U S H
N S B P H H C A E L B O W I H E
A P P O L I S H X E N E N P I D
E U R J O H N F R A D K A L N G
L U C E E M K G C A U R L I G E
C M B A W O L G P N K O B Q U C
M P R O V O N S B O R F I U P U
U S U D V I M L F R W L C D L T
U X S E R E O N N O E D H S I T
C A S E T C O P W B I T E R Q E
A E T O K R R H S A O U S R U R
V A L E O A B E I L L O C U I H
W C R A K Y R O C L E A N E D S
```

Answer on p177.

Here are some statements about the story of Martha and Mary. Mark a 'T' in the box for each one you think is true, and an 'F' for each one you think is false.

1. Jesus was a hard worker.

2. A woman called Mary invited Jesus into her house.

3. Mary had a sister called Margaret.

4. The two sisters had servants to do the housework for them.

5. As soon as Mary saw Jesus, she stopped what she was doing and sat down to listen to Him.

6. Jesus had lots to teach Martha and Mary.

7. Martha carried on working and didn't sit down with Jesus.

8. Mary was cross with Martha.

9. Martha complained to Jesus.

10. Mary stopped listening to Jesus and went to help Martha.

11. Jesus said that spending time with Him was the right thing to do.

12. Martha asked Jesus to give her a hand with the cleaning.

Answer on p177.

God's Love

Matthew 6

People. People everywhere. That's what it was like whenever Jesus was around. A mass of people. A seething, surging, super-sea of bodies. You should have seen the size of those crowds! Jesus just couldn't get away from them. They followed Him about nearly everywhere.

Not that He minded, of course. If there were people wanting to know about God, then Jesus wanted to talk to them. If there were people who were ill, or sad, or lonely, or worried – then Jesus just wanted to help them out.

There was one particular day when Jesus climbed a hill so that the super-sea of people could see and hear Him more easily, and He could see them more easily, too. He taught them about making God number one – putting God first, so that He's more important than anything else.

Jesus said, 'Do not store up riches for yourselves here on earth, where moths and rust destroy, and robbers break in and steal. Instead, store up riches for yourselves in heaven, where moths and rust cannot destroy, and robbers cannot break in and steal. For your heart will always be where your riches are' (6 v 19–21).

That's so true! Moths ate right through my mum's jumper. It totally fell apart when she got it out of the cupboard. And Dad's wheelbarrow turned rusty in the rain, so the wheel went wonky. AND – my friend had his skateboard stolen from outside the post office. So making God the most important part of your life, now that's something to rely on. Because God's love lasts forever.

Jesus said the same thing about money. 'No one can be a slave of two masters; he will hate one and love the other; he will be loyal to one and despise the other. You cannot serve both God and money' (6 v 24).

Not that Jesus meant there's anything wrong with being rich. The wrong part is the *wrong attitude*. If money is more important than God, then it gets in the way. It means people can't properly be friends with Him.

Then Jesus said, 'And anyway, why be fussed about money? Why worry about not having enough food to eat, or not having proper clothes to wear? Look around you. Do you see the birds? They don't spend their time growing their own food and storing it away. They don't worry about it. But God still takes care of them, doesn't He? And think how much more important you are to God than the birds – so of course He's going to take care of you too.'

Jesus added, 'And why worry about clothes? Look how the wild flowers grow: they do not work or make clothes for themselves. But I tell you that not even King Solomon with all his wealth had clothes as beautiful as one of these flowers … How little faith you have!' (6 v 28–30).

It's hard not to worry sometimes, though. Especially if you're a worrier-type person.

But Jesus said to remember that God loves us and knows what we need. So we have to try not to worry. Even if we are worrier-type people.

'Put God first,' Jesus said, 'talk to Him and try to live the way He wants you to, and let Him look after you.'

Then He smiled, 'So do not worry about tomorrow' (6 v 34).

The huge crowds at the foot of the hill stretched back further and further as the news spread that Jesus was teaching there. And more and more people learned from the greatest Teacher in the whole of history just how enormous God's love really is.

How well do you remember the story of Jesus telling people not to worry and about God's love? See if you can answer the questions and fill in the gaps without looking back!

1. What followed Jesus about nearly everywhere?

_____

2. What sort of people did Jesus want to help? I _ _, s _ _, l _ _ _ _ _ and w _ _ _ _ _ _ people.

3. Why did Jesus climb a hill?

_____

4. What did Jesus teach people to make God in their lives?

_____

5. What did Jesus say destroys things here on earth?

_____

6. Where did Jesus say is the best place to store up riches?

_____

7. What did Jesus say you can't serve at the same time?

_____

8. Jesus said: 'Why worry about not having enough _ _ _ _ _ _ _ _ _, or not having _ _ _ _ _ _ _ _ _ _ _ _ _ _ to wear?'

9. What doesn't worry about having enough food to eat?

_____

10. Which king's clothes weren't as beautiful as the flowers?

_____

11. God _ _ _ _ _ _ us and knows what we _ _ _ _ _.

12. Jesus said: 'So do not worry about _ _ _ _ _ _ _ _ _.'

Answer on p177.

In his letter to the Ephesians in the New Testament, you can find Paul's prayer for them. It talks about the amazing love that Jesus has for everyone.

Paul's prayer is for all of us, too. Here it is, but each word is back to front. Write them all out in the spaces the right way round. Then read the prayer a few times and think about the MASSIVENESS of Jesus' love for you!

'I yarp taht tsirhC lliw ekam sih emoh ni ruoy straeh hguorht htiaf. I yarp taht uoy yam evah ruoy stoor dna noitadnuof ni evol, os taht uoy, rehtegot htiw lla s'doG elpoep, yam evah eht rewop ot dnatsrednu woh daorb dna gnol, woh hgih dna peed, si s'tsirhC evol.' (snaisehpE 3 v 17–18)

Answer on p177.

The Seed Story

Mark 4

When Jesus was on the earth, He told different stories as a way to help people understand God and know how to live the way He wants them to.

One story He told was about a farmer who went out to sow some seeds in his fields.

'There was once a farmer who went out to sow some corn,' Jesus began. 'He trudged all over his field, scattering the seeds, and some of them fell onto the path. Well, the seeds on that pathway never got the chance to grow, because the birds spotted them. Down they swooped to scratch and peck in the dirt, until they'd eaten them all up.

'There were some other seeds,' Jesus went on, 'that fell in among stones where there wasn't much soil. The seeds sprouted quickly enough, but when the sun came up, its heat burnt the fresh, new shoots. And because there wasn't enough earth for their roots to grow down into, they quickly died.

'And still more of the seeds,' Jesus said, 'fell in among brambles. They grew, but the brambles did, too – and the brambles were too strong. They choked the farmer's plants so that they didn't produce any corn.'

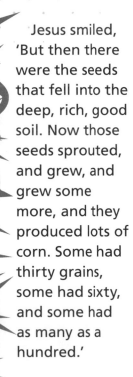

Jesus smiled, 'But then there were the seeds that fell into the deep, rich, good soil. Now those seeds sprouted, and grew, and grew some more, and they produced lots of corn. Some had thirty grains, some had sixty, and some had as many as a hundred.'

'Please, Jesus,' they said, 'please explain what You mean. Because we don't quite get it.'

Jesus said, 'Right, then. The sower sows God's message (4 v 14). But there are some people who are like the seeds that fell on the path and were eaten up by the birds. They hear the message, but they ignore it. They want to live the way *they* want, and not the way God wants. They don't want to share their lives with Him. They are the seeds that never even start to grow.'

Jesus went on, 'Other people are like the seeds that fall on rocky ground. As soon as they hear the message, they receive it gladly. But it does not sink deep into them, and they don't last long. So when trouble or persecution comes because of the message, they give up at once (4 v 16–17).

'And remember the seeds that landed in the brambles?' Jesus said. 'They are like people who also hear the message, but they spend so much time worrying, and trying to make money, and chasing after all the other things they want, that they never learn to trust God. They never really understand what it means to be friends with Him, so they don't discover what an amazing life He has planned for them.'

At last, Jesus got to the seeds that fell in the good earth. What sort of people were they? He explained, 'But other people are like the seeds sown in good soil. They hear the message, accept it, and bear fruit' (4 v 20).

Those are the people who love God and want to serve Him; who tell others about God, too, and know that they'll be with Him forever.

The seeds that are sown in God's good earth are like God's very best friends.

Here's a list of beautiful flowers that grow in God's good earth. Unscramble the letters to find out what they are.

1. Reos _____

2. yacinhtH _____

3. syaPn _____

4. upliT _____

5. Prorseim _____

6. terBtucup _____

7. Spdrngoaan _____

8. foDafdil _____

9. isDay _____

10. Cnwefloorr _____

11. Nicssarus _____

12. Gnieraum _____

Answer on p177.

Scattering
Grains
Seeds
Hundred
Field
Message
Birds
Ignore
Swooped
Sower
Sprouted
Gladly
Friends
Good
Rocky
Earth
Fruit
People
Brambles
Serve

Can you find these twenty words from the story about the seeds in the word search?

Answer on p177.

```
P E O P L E Y K C O R T S
F R I E N D S T I U R F E
S D S A I G N O R E H S R
D E N S E E D S G O T O V
L A I P H A S C N Y R W E
E H A R E U E E I L A E S
I U R O M N R I R D E R E
F N G U N E I I E A O S L
R D W T A R S P T L T D B
E R E E A R O S T G T R M
E E E D I O I O A O N I A
E D O W W R M O C G D B R
E A A S G O O D S L E T B
```

The One Who Came Back

Jesus did a lot of walking. There were so many places to visit that were all *full* of people who needed to hear about God. Jesus wanted to make sure He covered as much ground as He could.

Today was another walking day. Jesus was on His way to the city of Jerusalem.

Up ahead of Him was a village. It was as Jesus started towards the village that He noticed the men. There were ten of them. All in a huddle. And they seemed to be shuffling slowly towards Him, dragging their feet in the dust.

Suddenly, they stopped. All ten of them together.

Jesus peered at them and they stared back at Him. It only took a second for Him to realise why they had stopped. The men were sick. They had a terrible, terrible skin disease that was terribly, terribly easy to catch. So they had to keep away from other people. The only ones they were allowed to mix with were the ones who were sick like them – with the terrible disease.

But these men had heard about Jesus. They knew who He was as soon as they saw Him.

They stood at a distance and shouted, 'Jesus! Master! Take pity on us!' (17 v 12–13).

That's so scary! Jesus must have wondered if He'd end up with the disease, too.

I don't think Jesus was thinking about Himself. When He looked at the ten men, He wasn't scared, He was sad. They were ill and they were lonely. And they couldn't go home.

But Jesus knew that with God's power, He could change all that. Jesus knew He could make the men better.

He called over to them, 'Go and let the priests examine you' (17 v 14).

The men looked at each other. 'Odd,' they must have thought. 'We don't need a priest to tell us we're ill.'

But, they did as Jesus had told them to. They turned around and began to shuffle back the way they had come.

Suddenly, one man glanced at the man beside him – and gasped!

'You're better! You're better! Your skin – it's all better!'

The man with the all-better skin gulped back, 'And so is yours. Look! Look at yourself!'

'I'm looking!' cried yet another man. 'I'm looking and I'm all better, too!'

It was the same for all of them. They were *all* – all better! All ten men. From head to toe and toe to head, their skin was smooth and glowing and healthy. The disease had all gone.

The men were all gone, too. You couldn't see them for dust. They rushed off to find a priest who could pronounce that they were well again. Then they'd be allowed to go back to their families.

Well – when I say they were *all* gone – one of them didn't shoot off. One of them turned to see if there was any sign of Jesus somewhere behind him on the road.

When one of them saw that he was healed, he came back, praising God in a loud voice. He threw himself to the ground at Jesus' feet and thanked him (17 v 15–16).

It wasn't just a healthy body Jesus had given back to him. It was his life. His whole life! Because now he'd be allowed to go home.

Jesus said, 'There were ten men who were healed; where are the other nine?' (17 v 17).

He glanced up and along the road. It was empty. 'Why is it,' Jesus asked, 'that only one of you has come back to say thank You to God?'

But then Jesus smiled at the one man in front of Him. He said, 'Get up and go; your faith has made you well' (17 v 19).

Look closely at these pictures of ten men. They may all look exactly the same, but one of them is slightly different. Can you spot the odd one out?

Answer on p178.

How well can you remember the story of the ten men and the one who was thankful? Work out the missing words and fill in the crossword.

1. _ _ _ _ _ was walking to Jerusalem.

2. Jesus saw _ _ _ men coming towards Him.

3. The men had a terrible skin _ _ _ _ _ _ _. They asked Jesus for help.

4. Unlike other people, Jesus was not _ _ _ _ _ _ of the men.

5. Jesus told the men to go and find _ _ _ _ _ _ _.

6. On the way, the men were _ _ _ _ _ _.

7. Out of the ten men, only _ _ _ went back to say 'Thank You' to Jesus.

8. Jesus said, 'Your _ _ _ _ _ has made you well.'

Answer on p178.

The Water-Walker

Matthew 14

I've never climbed up a hill specially to pray. I'm going to do that. Soon ... As soon as I can find a hill ... Wait! I live in Holly Hill. Perfect!

Did you know that Jesus got tired sometimes? I mean, it's not surprising, is it? He walked for miles and miles, travelling from place to place. There were always crowds of people following Him around; people who needed His help, people who wanted Him to teach them. People who just wanted to be close to Him. Jesus didn't get much time to relax and have a rest. So of course He got tired. I know *I* would.

But He did need time to Himself, just like we do. And having time on His own with God was really important to Jesus, too. Time to talk to Him, as well as to listen to Him. Time to be refreshed by Him. Jesus wanted to feel totally connected to His Father God every single moment.

One evening, after Jesus had been working especially hard with people for God, He made the disciples get into the boat and go on ahead to the other side of the lake, while he sent the people away (14 v 22). Then He climbed up a hill all by Himself so that He could spend some time praying. Just Him and God.

Jesus stayed on the hill for a long time. Right through the evening, and on into the night. And when at last He'd finished talking to God, it was quite dark.

He peered across the water. He could only just make out His friends in their boat on the lake. It looked as if they were having a bit of a rough time. A wind had sprung up and the boat was bouncing about all over the place.

Jesus got up, strolled down the hill, and went to meet it. But not in another boat. Oh no. Jesus WALKED.
ON THE WATER!
I *know*, right?!

With the bad weather closing in, Jesus' friends already had quite a lot to cope with just keeping the boat upright. And then all at once – they saw Jesus. Only they didn't realise it was Jesus. They didn't think it was a proper person. Well, you wouldn't, would you? Jesus was, after all, *walking on the water*.

They stared at Him and they were terrified. 'It's a ghost!' they said, and screamed with fear. Jesus spoke to them at once. 'Courage!' he said. 'It is I! Don't be afraid!' (14 v 26–27).

Still they couldn't take their eyes off Him. It was Peter who was the first to speak. 'Lord, if it is really you, order me to come out on the water to you' (14 v 28).

So Jesus did. 'Come on then, Peter,' He called.

Peter hitched up his robe. Was he scared? He must have been a bit scared! But he could see Jesus. Right there, standing on the water. And up he climbed – up and over the side of the boat. Down and down until his feet touched the

water, too … Until his feet touched the water and he began *to walk on it!*

It was all going stonkingly well!

But then, suddenly – Peter got distracted. By the howling wind and by the churning waves. He took His eyes off Jesus and he began to sink. He splashed and kicked and thrashed about, but the only way he was going was down!

'Save me, Lord!' he cried. At once Jesus reached out and grabbed hold of him and said, 'How little faith you have! Why did you doubt?' (14 v 30–31).

With Jesus' help, Peter scrambled back into the boat. Jesus climbed up behind him. Which is when something else amazing happened. The wind stopped blowing. The water stopped churning.

All was calm.

Then the disciples in the boat worshipped Jesus. 'Truly you are the Son of God!' they exclaimed (14 v 33).

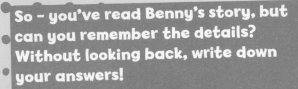

So – you've read Benny's story, but can you remember the details? Without looking back, write down your answers!

1. Why did Jesus get tired?

2. What was really important to Jesus?

3. What did Jesus tell His disciples to do?

4. Where did Jesus go to pray one evening?

5. When Jesus had finished talking to God, what was the weather like?

6. How did Jesus get out to the disciples' boat?

7. What did the disciples think Jesus was when they first spotted Him in the storm?

8. Who stepped out of the boat to go to Jesus?

9. Why did this disciple start to sink?

10. What did Jesus do when He saw that His friend was in trouble?

11. What happened as soon as Jesus was back in the boat?

12. Who did Jesus' disciples say that He was?

Answer on p178.

No matter what happens, or how difficult things sometimes seem to be, the Bible gives us some astonishing and fabulous encouragement! Crack the code to find out what it is and where to find it in the Bible, and write it out in the spaces below.

A	B	C	D	E	F	G	H	I	J	K	L	M
◬	▢	◐	▷	▽	▶	☉	▷	▢	◁	⊘	⊟	△

N	O	P	Q	R	S	T	U	V	W	X	Y	Z
⊠	▽	▷	▷	◁	◀	⊕	⊡	◀	⊟	⊖	⊞	◁

'⊕▷▽ ⊟▽◁▷ ▢◁ ◬⊞ ▷▽⊟▷▽◁,

_____

▢ ⊡▢⊟⊟ ⊠▽⊕ ▢▽ ◬▷◁◬▢▷▷.

_____

⊡▷◬⊕ ◐◬⊠ ◬⊠⊟▽⊠▽ ▷▽

_____

⊕▽ ◬▽?' (▷▽▢◁▽⊡◁ 13 ◁ 6)

_____

Cracked it? Now learn the verse by heart, so that you can say it to yourself if you're ever faced with something scary.

Answer on p178.

Alive and Well!

John 11

Jesus had a good friend called Lazarus. He was friends with Lazarus' sisters, Martha and Mary, too. Jesus was with His disciples when a message from the two sisters was brought to Him: 'Lord, your dear friend is ill' (11 v 3).

If someone told me one of the Topz Gang was ill, I'd be round there like a shot. Obviously Jesus couldn't get to any places like a shot, because of having to walk everywhere. But when He heard the sad news, He didn't even get going straightaway.

He just said, 'Lazarus' illness won't end with him dying. This has happened to bring glory to God. It will bring glory to me, too.'

It was two whole days before Jesus finally said to His disciple friends, 'Right. Time to go to Lazarus. He's fallen asleep and I need to wake him up.'

Jesus' friends shrugged their shoulders. 'Well, if Lazarus is asleep, that's a good thing. Sleeping helps you get better.'

But they hadn't understood what Jesus meant.

So He told them, 'Lazarus is dead, but for your sake I am glad that I was not with him, so that you will believe. Let us go to him' (11 v 14–15).

That's so weird. Why wouldn't Jesus have wanted to visit His friend while he was ill? I mean, Jesus can work miracles. He could have stopped Lazarus from dying in the first place.

When Martha heard that Jesus was nearly there, she went out to meet Him. And Martha said the very same thing. 'If you had been here, Lord, my brother would not have died!' (11 v 21). You see, by the time Jesus arrived, Lazarus had already been buried for four days.

But although Martha was heartbroken to have lost her brother, she still believed that Jesus could put things right somehow. She still hung on to her faith in Him.

She added, 'But I know that even now God will give you whatever you ask him for' (11 v 22).

Jesus replied with something amazing: 'I am the resurrection and the life. Those who believe in me will live, even though they die; and all those who live and believe in me will never die' (11 v 25–26).

Martha went to fetch her sister, Mary. Mary was in floods of tears and hurried out to meet Jesus. The people who had come to comfort the sisters went with her. They were crying, too.

'Where have you buried Lazarus?' Jesus asked.

Someone answered, 'Come with us and we'll show You.'

Then the tears fell from Jesus' eyes for Lazarus.

'See how much he loved him!' the people said (11 v 36).

But there were others who seemed cross with Jesus. 'If He could make a blind man see,' they grumbled to each other, 'then how come He couldn't stop Lazarus from dying?'

Jesus stood in front of His friend's grave. It was a cave in a rock, and a stone had been rolled across the entrance.

Jesus ordered: 'Take that stone out of the way.'

Martha peered at Him anxiously. She shook her head. 'But we can't do that, Lord. Lazarus has been dead for four days. The smell will be awful.'

Jesus said to her, 'Didn't I tell you that you would see God's glory if you believed?' (11 v 40).

With a lot of heaving and shoving, the little crowd of people managed to move the stone away from the tomb entrance.

And what Jesus did then was pray: 'I thank you, Father, that you listen to me. I know that you always listen to me, but I say this for the sake of the people here, so that they will believe that you sent me.' After he had said this, he called out in a loud voice, 'Lazarus, come out!' (11 v 41–43).

There was a moment.
The teeniest of moments.
And then Lazarus appeared.
Walking on his own two feet
out of the tomb.
Tall and strong and healthy.
Jesus, 'the Resurrection', had
brought him back to life.

Friends
Martha
Illness
Glory
Asleep
Lazarus
Believe
Buried
Heartbroken
Brother
Faith
Jesus
Mary
Sisters
Resurrection
Life
Tears
Comfort
Loved
Father

D	M	A	R	T	H	A	B	A	R	I	O	L
B	S	R	E	T	S	I	S	R	R	I	O	I
B	U	R	I	E	D	A	A	E	S	I	N	F
N	O	I	T	C	E	R	R	U	S	E	R	E
E	M	A	R	Y	S	B	A	F	K	Y	S	J
B	F	E	E	H	E	A	L	O	R	U	E	C
R	E	R	E	L	S	L	R	O	R	S	O	S
O	E	E	I	L	R	B	L	A	U	M	R	S
T	L	E	E	T	G	Z	S	F	A	T	E
H	V	E	H	R	N	A	R	O	E	I	N
E	P	T	A	A	L	D	R	T	R	O	L	L
R	A	E	E	O	J	T	S	D	E	V	O	L
F	H	J	E	H	T	I	A	F	O	O	T	I

Answer on p178.

Read these statements about the story of Lazarus. Mark a 'T' in the box for each one you think is true, and an 'F' for each one you think is false.

1. Jesus' disciples sent Him a message about Lazarus.

2. As soon as Jesus knew that Lazarus was ill, He went to visit him.

3. Lazarus' illness would bring glory to God.

4. Lazarus was Mary and Martha's cousin.

5. When Jesus arrived, Lazarus had been buried for three days.

6. People had come to visit Martha and Mary to comfort them.

7. Some people grumbled that Jesus hadn't kept Lazarus from dying.

8. At Lazarus' tomb, Jesus said, 'Whatever you do, don't move the stone out of the way.'

9. Jesus prayed to God outside Lazarus' tomb.

10. Jesus knew that God always listened to Him.

11. Jesus told Lazarus to stay where he was.

12. At Jesus' command, Lazarus walked out of the tomb, alive and well.

The Fantastic Party

Luke 14

Jesus was just the BEST storyteller in the entire whole world of storytelling. Not only are His stories very cool, but they all mean something, too. They have really important things to teach us about God – about how to live His way and share our lives with Him.

There was one story Jesus told about a party.

Wooo! I love a good party. I like that pass-the-parcel game. I've never actually won it, but it's pretty cool waiting to see if I'm going to. And I don't even mind not winning. Unless Sarah wins, of course, in which case I mind a lot. But it's OK because I'm always way better than she is at karaoke! So anyway, is there cake at this party?

Probably. Jesus called it a 'feast'. So it was going to be huge and brilliant! Plenty to eat, plenty to drink. Maybe even some music.

Jesus said, 'The man who had decided to hold the feast invited lots and lots of people. This was going to be a party to end all parties! He made sure everything was ready – all laid out magnificently for his guests – and then, he sent his servant out to the people he'd invited to tell them that it was time. The party was about to begin.'

So, what a let-down it was when, one after the other, the guests started making up excuses for why they couldn't come.

Jesus went on, 'The first one told the servant, "I have bought a field and must go and look at it; please accept my apologies." Another one said, "I have bought five pairs of oxen and am on my way to try them out; please accept my apologies." Another one said, "I have just got married, and for that reason I cannot come"' (14 v 18–20).

So weird. Imagine turning down the chance to go to such a fantastic party!

And now there were no guests – not a single one – coming to enjoy it.

Well, when the servant went back to his master to tell him what all the people who were supposed to be coming had said, he wasn't happy. Not happy one bit. I mean, you wouldn't be, would you? Not after all that effort.

Jesus went on, 'The master was furious and said to his servant, "Hurry out to the streets and alleys of the town, and bring back the poor, the crippled, the blind, and the lame"' (14 v 21).

So away went the servant again. He did exactly as he was told. He went to look for people who were poor and people who were ill; people who couldn't walk and people who couldn't see. He searched out all the people no one else cared about.

'And all *those* people,' Jesus said, 'they grabbed the chance to go to the party – because what an amazing chance it was! But even with all of those guests, there was still room for more.

'So the master said to the servant, "Go out to the country roads and lanes and make people come in, so that my house will be full. I tell you all that none of those who were invited will taste my dinner!"' (14 v 23–24).

'You see, the master,' said Jesus, 'wanted his house to be full of people who were happy to have been asked to the party. Who were excited to go and ready to enjoy all the good things there.'

I bet they did enjoy themselves, too.

And that's exactly what God wants for us. He invites EVERYONE to come to His party! He calls to ALL OF US to come to Him and be His friends!

Then we can be with Him forever – living an amazing life with God, which starts right now. The very minute we say: 'I hear You, God. Thank You. Yes, please!'

Topz are throwing a party! They've made a list of the food and everything else they're going to need. Unscramble the words below and write them in the spaces to find out how to party Topz-style!

1. deLenamo _____

2. ispCrs _____

3. Bloalons _____

4. gSasaeus no scksti _____

5. cle acerm _____

6. yPrta ppersop _____

7. sCeehy cuitbiss _____

8. aspreG _____

9. Gmeas _____

10. Fraiy akces _____

11. sMuic _____

12. aJm swahesndic _____

Answer on p178.

Jesus gives us some wonderful invitations to come to Him in the Bible. Here is one of them. Cross out every q, x and z to find out what it is, and write it out in the space below.

'Lzxqiqstzzexnx! I xzsqqtanxzqdx qaxtz zxtqhzez xxdxoqzorq

_____

zaxnqdq qqkxnqozckxx; zqiqfq xaznqyqqoxxnzez qhzexaxrqszz

_____

qzxmqzxyqzx vxoxxiqzczeq qazznxqdz zxopeqnzsz xtzheq

_____

zdoxxoqrz, I zwqixlxlq xcqozmzzeq qinx qqanxdz exatz qwixthzx

_____

ztzhxeqxmq, anxdq xxtqzhezyxq qzwilxql xezaqtx zqwxiqztxhx

_____

xmzeq.' (Rqzevxezlxxaqztzqioxnz 3 v 20)

Answer on p178.

Have you said yes to Jesus' invitation yet?

147

Jesus in Jerusalem

Luke 19 and John 14

Jesus was always on the move. He wanted to reach as many villages and towns as He could so that He could tell people how much God loved them and wanted to share their lives.

As it got near to Passover festival time, Jesus and His disciples made their way to Jerusalem. The Passover was a time for God's people to get together and celebrate all that God had given to them and had done for them. Jesus planned to share the special Passover meal with His friends.

When they'd nearly reached the city, Jesus turned to two of His disciples.

He said, 'Go to the village there ahead of you; as you go in, you will find a colt tied up that has never been ridden. Untie it and bring it here. If someone asks you why you are untying it, tell him that the Master needs it' (Luke 19 v 30–31).

The two disciples did as Jesus had said. They found the village, and almost straightaway, they spotted the young donkey.

Some people did ask why they were taking it. So, just as Jesus had told them to, His two friends said, 'The Master needs it.' Then they led the donkey to Jesus. They took off their cloaks, laid them across the rough hair of the donkey's back, and helped Jesus to climb on.

And that's how Jesus arrived in Jerusalem. Riding on that little donkey.

There were people everywhere to see Jesus. They'd heard He was on His way. They rushed out to line the streets as He rode by. They cheered and shouted, and made such a fuss of Him. Well, of course they did – He's the Son of God! They threw their cloaks on the road for the donkey to walk on, and they waved tall leaves from palm trees.

Jesus is written about in the Old Testament. Did you know that? He was written about way before He was even born. Those writings are called 'prophecies'. And one prophet called Zechariah wrote that Jesus would arrive in Jerusalem riding on a donkey!

They began to thank God and praise him in loud voices for all the great things that they had seen: 'God bless the king who comes in the name of the Lord! Peace in heaven and glory to God!' (Luke 19 v 37–38).

Not everyone was in such a good mood, though. There were some Pharisees in the crowds watching Jesus, too. Pharisees were teachers, like Jesus. But they didn't teach like Jesus. All they cared about was following rules, and punishing people who didn't follow their rules. They hated Jesus for teaching about God's love and forgiveness.

When they heard all the shouting, they snarled at Him, 'Order these people to be quiet!'

But how could anyone who believes in the Son of God be quiet when He's right there in front of them?!

Jesus answered, 'I tell you that if they keep quiet, the stones themselves will start shouting' (Luke 19 v 40).

When it was almost time for the Passover festival, Jesus and His friends sat together in a house in the city. The festival should have been a time to be happy and to celebrate. But Jesus was quiet. Thoughtful. Deep down inside Him, He seemed to be very sad.

'I have to go away soon,' He said. 'I have to leave you. Believe in God and believe also in me. There are many rooms in my Father's house, and I am going to prepare a place for you. I would not tell you this if it were not so. And after I go and prepare a place for you, I will come back and take you to myself, so that you will be where I am' (John 14 v 1–3).

Jesus knew He had enemies. He knew there were people who hated Him and were plotting to kill Him.

But He also knew that soon He would be with His Father in heaven and, one day, we will be there with Him, too!

Just as Danny said, there are lots of prophecies about Jesus in the Old Testament. Here's the prophecy Danny mentions. You'll have to crack the code to fill in the missing words.

A	B	C	D	E	F	G	H	I	J	K	L	M
△	⊠	◍	▷	▽	▷	⊙	▷	□	◁	☑	⊞	△

N	O	P	Q	R	S	T	U	V	W	X	Y	Z
⊠	▽	▽	◁	◁	◁	⊕	⊙	◁	⊟	⊖	⊞	◁

'◁▷▽⊙⊕ for joy,
you ▷▽▷▷⊟▽ of
◁▽◁⊙◁△⊟▽! Look,
your ☑□⊠⊙ is coming
to ⊞▽⊙! He comes
⊕◁□□◁△▷▷△⊠⊕ and
◁□◍⊕▽◁□▽◍◁,
but ▷□△⊠⊟△
and ◁□▷□⊠⊙
on a ▷▽⊠▷△⊞'
(◁▽◍▷△◁□△▷ 9 v 9).

'_ _ _ _ _ _ for joy,

you _ _ _ _ _ _ _ _ of

_ _ _ _ _ _ _ _ _ _ _ _! Look,

your _ _ _ _ _ is coming

to _ _ _ _! He comes

_ _ _ _ _ _ _ _ _ _ _ _ and

_ _ _ _ _ _ _ _ _ _ _ _ , but

_ _ _ _ _ _ _ and _ _ _ _ _ _ _ _

on a _ _ _ _ _ _ _ _ ',

(_ _ _ _ _ _ _ _ _ _ _ 9 v 9).

Answer on p179.

Now read the verse through and think how amazing it is that it was written nearly 500 years before Jesus was even born!

Jesus told His disciple friends that He was going to be with His Father in heaven. He promised that one day they would be with Him there, too. That promise is also for us! But what must we do to get to spend forever with Jesus in heaven? Find your way through the maze to Jesus and read the words you discover along the right path.

YOU

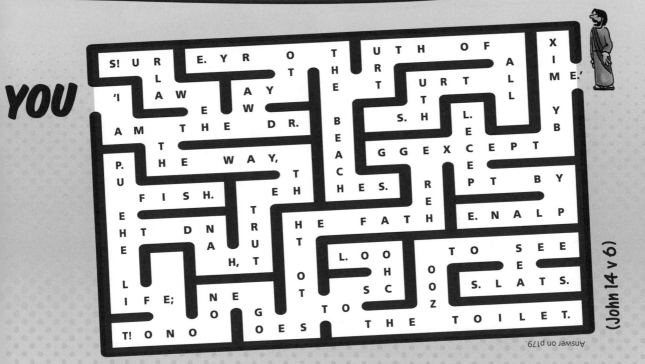

(John 14 v 6)

Answer on p179.

Jesus is the way! If we believe that Jesus is God's Son and follow Him, we will be with Him in heaven one day!

God's Great Plan

Mark 14 and 15, Luke 22 and John 14

It was the first day of the Passover festival. Jesus asked two of His disciples to get everything ready. Then, that evening, He sat down to a meal with all His friends.

While they were eating, Jesus took a piece of bread, gave a prayer of thanks, broke it, and gave it to his disciples. 'Take it,' he said (Mark 14 v 22). 'Eat this bread, and remember me always.'

Then Jesus picked up His cup of wine, gave thanks to God, and handed it to them; and they all drank from it (Mark 14 v 23). 'Remember me when you drink this wine, too,' He said. 'This will remind you that my death is for each one of you – for all people – so that God can forgive everyone for the wrong things they have done.'

That's what we do in church. We share bread and we drink from a special cup, to remember how Jesus died for us.

Jesus told His friends that He had to go away soon, but that they wouldn't be left on their own. He said, 'I will ask the Father, and he will give you another Helper, who will stay with you for ever … The Helper, the Holy Spirit, whom the Father will send in my name, will teach you everything and make you remember all that I have told you' (John 14 v 16, 26).

Jesus' friends loved Him so much. It was hard for them to sit and listen to Him telling them that He had to die.

It was hard for them to understand it all, too, even though Jesus explained it: how people couldn't be friends with God anymore because of all the wrong things they had done. How they deserved to be punished. But how God had sent His only Son, Jesus, to the earth to take the punishment instead.

To die to take away all those wrong things.

To die to bring people back to God.

When Jesus and His friends had finished their meal, they went out into the night for a walk. They went into a garden called Gethsemane, and Jesus spent some time there, talking to God.

But He hadn't been there long when suddenly, there was a noise. There were voices. A crowd of people pushed their way into the garden. A man called Judas was there. Why was he with them? He used to be one of Jesus' disciple friends.

But he wasn't a friend tonight.

He said to the men with him, 'The man I kiss is the one you want. Arrest him and take him away under guard' (Mark 14 v 44).

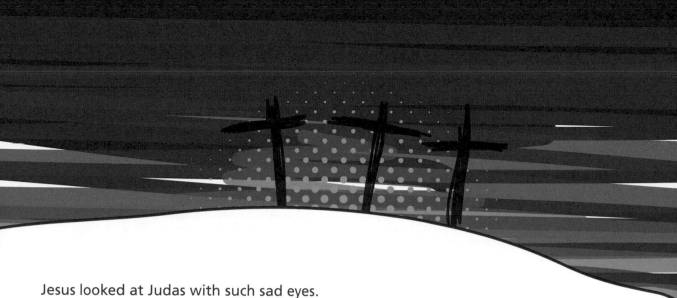

Jesus looked at Judas with such sad eyes. He said, 'Judas, is it with a kiss that you betray the Son of Man?' (Luke 22 v 48).

And it was. That was how Jesus was arrested. Through a kiss.

Jesus was taken to the high priest, who asked Him, 'Are you the Messiah, the Son of the Blessed God?' 'I am,' answered Jesus (Mark 14 v 61–62).

'No one can say such a thing!' shouted the high priest. 'It is disrespectful. It is an insult to God!'

The men who hated Jesus wouldn't believe what He said. They didn't *want* to believe Him. They all voted against him: he was guilty and should be put to death (Mark 14 v 64).

So the soldiers grabbed hold of Jesus and dragged Him away. They spat on Him and they beat Him. They wove together a crown out of thorny branches and they stuck it on His head.

And when they'd done all of that, they crucified Him. They nailed Him to a wooden cross.

At noon the whole country was covered with darkness, which lasted for three hours (Mark 15 v 33).

Then Jesus cried out. He called to His Father God: 'My God, my God, why did you abandon me?' (Mark 15 v 34).

And He died.

It was awful. What a horrible, horrible day.

But it wasn't the end. God's great plan was not finished …

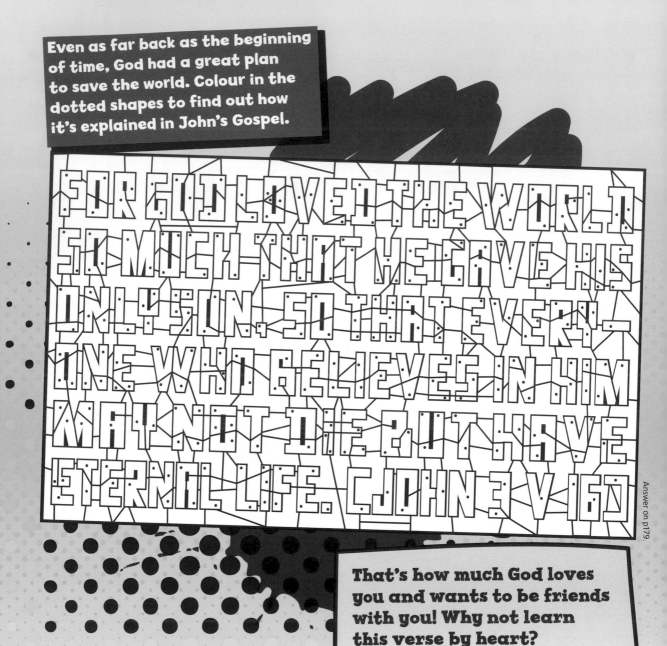

Even as far back as the beginning of time, God had a great plan to save the world. Colour in the dotted shapes to find out how it's explained in John's Gospel.

FOR GOD LOVED THE WORLD SO MUCH THAT HE GAVE HIS ONLY SON, SO THAT EVERY-ONE WHO BELIEVES IN HIM MAY NOT DIE BUT HAVE ETERNAL LIFE. (JOHN 3 V 16)

Answer on p179.

That's how much God loves you and wants to be friends with you! Why not learn this verse by heart?

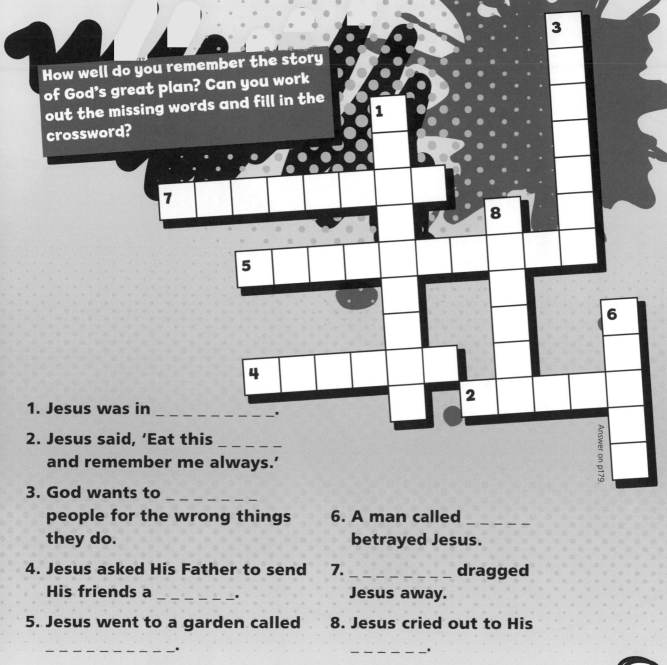

How well do you remember the story of God's great plan? Can you work out the missing words and fill in the crossword?

1. Jesus was in _ _ _ _ _ _ _ _ _ _.

2. Jesus said, 'Eat this _ _ _ _ _ and remember me always.'

3. God wants to _ _ _ _ _ _ _ _ people for the wrong things they do.

4. Jesus asked His Father to send His friends a _ _ _ _ _ _.

5. Jesus went to a garden called _ _ _ _ _ _ _ _ _ _.

6. A man called _ _ _ _ _ _ betrayed Jesus.

7. _ _ _ _ _ _ _ _ _ dragged Jesus away.

8. Jesus cried out to His _ _ _ _ _ _.

Answer on p179.

Out of the Tomb!

On the first Sunday morning after Jesus had died, two of His friends, Mary Magdalene and another woman called Mary, went to the tomb where His body had been laid.

I bet they never expected THIS to happen when they got there:

Suddenly there was a violent earthquake; an angel of the Lord came down from heaven, rolled the stone away [from the entrance to the tomb], and sat on it. His appearance was like lightning, and his clothes were white as snow (28 v 2–3).

The two Marys must have been scared silly! The guards who'd been posted outside the tomb certainly were. They fainted flat out!

The angel spoke to the women. 'You must not be afraid,' he said. 'I know you are looking for Jesus, who was crucified. He is not here; he has been raised, just as he said' (28 v 5–6).

> I don't know about you, but I know what I'd have thought: *Raised? What are you talking about – raised?*

The angel said, 'Go quickly now, and tell his disciples, "He has been raised from death, and now he is going to Galilee ahead of you; there you will see him!" Remember what I have told you' (28 v 7).

Remember? As if the two Marys were likely to forget that! Anyway, off they hurtled to find Jesus' friends and give them the news.

Well – I bet they never expected *THIS* to happen either.

Suddenly – right there in front of them – stood Jesus!

'Peace be with you,' He said. And all they could do was fall down onto their knees in total shock and amazement, and worship Him.

'Do not be afraid,' Jesus said to them. 'Go and tell my brothers to go to Galilee, and there they will see me' (28 v 10).

And didn't the two Marys run! Faster than they'd ever run before. Faster than they probably thought they ever *could* run! They didn't stop until they'd found the disciples.

All out of breath, and probably not making too much sense, they gave Jesus' friends His message: Go to Galilee. That's where Jesus will meet you.

So that's where Jesus' friends went. I bet they set off running as fast as they could, too, with all sorts of questions flashing through their heads. Would Jesus be there yet? Was He still on His way? Would He wait for them? Was this even *real*?

But on a hill in Galilee, that's where they saw Him. Out of His tomb. Risen from the dead. Smiling at them.

Just like the two Marys, what else could the friends do but fall to the ground and worship Him.

'I've got some very important work for you to do,' Jesus said. 'I have been given all authority in heaven and on earth. Go, then, to all peoples everywhere and make them my disciples: baptize them in the name of the Father, the Son, and the Holy Spirit, and teach them to obey everything I have commanded you. And I will be with you always, to the end of the age' (28 v 18–20).

Always – do you hear that? What a promise!

It was now the disciples' job to tell as many people as they possibly could about Jesus. About what He had done. That He had made it possible for everyone to be forgiven by God; for everyone to be His friends again.

And that's our job now, too.

So that's how, shortly after the horrible, horrible day, came the greatest day in the history of the universe. The day when Jesus Christ, the Son of God, beat death and was brought back to amazing, incredible, lively, living LIFE!

These two guards look very similar, but there are ten differences between the two pictures. Can you spot them all?

Answer on p179.

1. When did the two Marys go to visit Jesus' tomb?

_____

2. First something 'violent' happened. What was it?

_____

3. Next, who suddenly appeared outside the tomb dressed in snow-white clothes?

_____

4. What was rolled away?

_____

5. The guards were terrified! What did they do?

_____

6. What were the two Marys told had happened to Jesus?

_____

7. What was the first thing Jesus said to the two Marys?

_____

8. What did the two Marys do when they saw Jesus?

_____

9. Jesus told the two Marys to give His friends (His 'brothers') a message. What was it?

_____

10. Where in Galilee did Jesus meet His friends?

_____

11. What was the special job Jesus wanted His friends to do?

_____

12. How long has Jesus promised to be with us for?

Answer on p179.

165

Jesus' Promise

Acts 1 and 2

Jesus – the amazing, incredible, lively, living, LIFE-full Jesus! – didn't just visit His disciples once. Oh no! For forty days after his death he appeared to them many times in ways that proved beyond doubt that he was alive (1 v 3).

Every time He was with them, He taught them even more about God. And even more about God's kingdom; God's family. How everyone could belong to God forever if they would only believe that He was God's Son, and follow Him.

Then came Jesus' very last day on the earth.

Jesus had given His friends an order: 'Do not leave Jerusalem, but wait for the gift I told you about, the gift my Father promised ... when the Holy Spirit comes upon you, you will be filled with power, and you will be witnesses for me ... to the ends of the earth' (1 v 4, 8).

When He'd finished speaking, a most wonderful thing happened. The disciples had already seen so many, many wonderful things – but even so, this took their breath away.

As they stood watching Jesus, He was gently lifted up and up and up into the sky. Into heaven. And then a cloud crossed His upwards pathway so that He was covered, and they weren't able to see Him anymore.

But they couldn't drag their eyes away. The sky was empty, yet still they stared and stared.

Jesus' friends didn't see them appear, but suddenly there were two men, dressed all in white, standing beside them.

'Why are you gazing up into the sky like that?' the men asked. 'Jesus has been taken up into heaven. It's time for Him to be with His Father. But one day, He'll come back!' they smiled. 'In just the same way as you've seen Him go.'

Jesus had told His friends to go back to Jerusalem and wait there until God sent the Holy Spirit to them.

So that's what they did. They wouldn't have known what to expect. They probably felt sad and lonely because Jesus now seemed to be gone from them.

They must have felt confused, too. Jesus was with them, then He wasn't because He died. Then He was with them again because He came back to life. But now He was gone – again! That's a lot to get your head round.

Yes, it is. And all they could do was trust Him. Trust in His promise.

And wait.

Until one day – when the Spirit came. The Spirit of God!

All Jesus' friends were gathered together in one place. Suddenly there was a noise from the sky which sounded like a strong wind blowing, and it filled the whole house where they were sitting. Then they saw what looked like tongues of fire which spread out and touched each person there (2 v 1–3).

The Holy Spirit filled them!

He filled them with courage. He filled them with strength. He filled them with the ability to speak in different languages, so that even more people could understand what they had to say about Jesus.

And out of their mouths poured God! Everything He is and everything He had done! The Spirit gave them the words – and they talked!

Jesus had kept His promise. He hadn't left them alone. The Holy Spirit was their new Helper.

Yes! And the Holy Spirit made them brave and excited and determined to spread the good news that Jesus had died and risen to save the world!

THE WHOLE WORLD.

The Holy Spirit would be with them every day to remind them that God was right by their sides.

He's with us, too.

Today.

Tomorrow.

Always.

Here are some statements about Josie's story. Mark a 'T' in the box for each one you think is true, and an 'F' for each one you think is false.

1. Jesus visited His disciples many times for forty days. ☐

2. Jesus taught His friends more and more about God and how to be a part of His family. ☐

3. Jesus told His friends to leave Jerusalem. ☐

4. Jesus told His friends to wait for the gift that God would send to them. ☐

5. The Holy Spirit would fill the disciples with power. ☐

6. Jesus was carried up to heaven by a crowd of angels. ☐

7. A huge bird flew in front of Jesus and hid Him from His friends. ☐

8. Three men told the disciples where Jesus had gone. ☐

9. When the Holy Spirit came, there was the sound of a strong wind, and tongues of fire touched the disciples. ☐

10. With the Holy Spirit inside them, no one could understand a word the disciples said. ☐

11. The Holy Spirit was the disciples' new Helper. ☐

12. The Holy Spirit would always remind the disciples that they were on their own now. ☐

Answer on p179.

The news that Jesus came to earth to bring us all back to God is too good to keep to ourselves! Here's something to remind you just how good this news actually is.

All the words are back to front. Write them in the spaces the right way round and read the amazing message of the New Testament.

htiW suseJ EDISEB su dna eht

yloH tiripS EDISNI su, ew era

reven no ruo nwo. eW era trap

fo s'doG ylimaf reverof dna reve!

Answer on p179.

Old Testament Activity Answers

The Very Beginning (Pages 12–13)

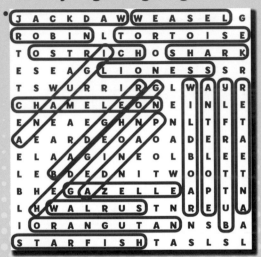

- 1. Magnificent 2. Awesome 3. Beautiful
  4. Brilliant 5. Powerful 6. Marvellous 7. Huge
  8. Spectacular 9. Stunning 10. Wonderful
  11. Fantastic 12. Splendid

In God's Garden (Pages 18–19)

- 1. Pineapple 2. Strawberry 3. Banana
  4. Orange 5. Raspberry 6. Apricot
  7. Blackcurrant 8. Watermelon 9. Blackberry
  10. Apple 11. Gooseberry 12. Pear

When the Rain Came Down (Pages 24–25)

- 'Noah did everything that the LORD commanded.' (Genesis 7 v 5)
- 1. A mess and a muddle 2. Good
  3. Good timber 4. Rooms 5. Tar 6. Forty days and forty nights 7. A dove 8. Three
  9. The water had started to go down
  10. Twice 11. As a sign that He would never again destroy the earth with a flood
  12. Because he trusted God

God's Good Friends (Pages 30–31)

- Abraham was a <u>good</u> man. He <u>trusted</u> God to do what was <u>best</u> for him and his <u>wife</u>, Sarah, and he always followed His <u>instructions</u>. God promised Abraham: 'I will <u>bless</u> you and give you many <u>descendants</u>.'

Abraham and Sarah found God's <u>promise</u> difficult to believe, but nothing is too <u>hard</u> for God. And God <u>never</u> <u>breaks</u> a promise.

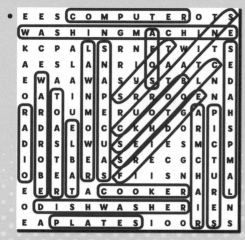

The Wrong Son (Pages 36–37)

- 1. Onion 2. Potato 3. Rhubarb 4. Carrot
  5. Coffee 6. Parsnip 7. Leek 8. Custard
  9. Lemonade 10. Parsley 11. Banana
  12. Chocolate
  Wrong ingredients: 3, 5, 8, 9, 11, 12

Moses, God's Hero (Pages 42–43)

- 1. False 2. False 3. True 4. False 5. True
  6. False 7. False 8. True 9. True 10. False
  11. False 12. True
- God uses ordinary people to do extraordinary things. Everyone is special to Him.

Spies in Canaan (Pages 48–49)

- 1. Wherever you go 2. The land of Canaan
  3. Two 4. In Rahab's house 5. The king
  6. At sunset 7. Up on the roof 8. Terrified
  9. Her father and mother, brothers and sisters and all their families 10. She lowered them out of her window with a rope
  11. A red cord 12. Three days

Gideon, the Brave and Mighty (Pages 54–55)

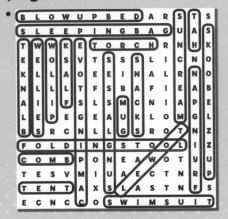

• God has promised to give us victory over our enemies. Do exactly as I do and we will defeat them.

A Baby for Hannah (Pages 60–61)

• 1. True 2. False 3. False 4. True 5. False 6. True 7. True 8. False 9. False 10. True 11. False 12. False

• 1. Rattle 2. Picture book 3. Booties 4. Hat 5. Teddy 6. Cuddly bunny 7. Cot mobile 8. Blanket 9. Changing mat 10. Baby bath 11. Night light 12. Rubber duck

A New King (Pages 66–67)

• God said to Samuel: 'I am sorry that I made Saul king; he has turned away from me and disobeyed my commands.' Samuel said to Saul: 'The LORD has torn the kingdom of Israel away from you today … God does not lie or change his mind.'

Solomon, the Wise (Pages 72–73)

• Benny: world's biggest bar of chocolate, Dave: bicycle helmet, Sarah: cat poster, Paul: computer game, Danny: running shoes, Josie: roller skates, John: football

Nehemiah Builds a New City (Pages 78–79)

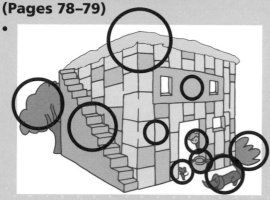

• Why did Nehemiah's plans succeed? Because he trusted God every step of the way.

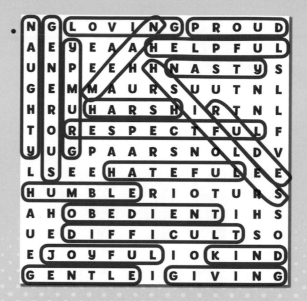

The Man God Chose (Pages 84–85)

- 1. True 2. False 3. False 4. True 5. False
  6. True 7. True 8. False 9. False 10. True
  11. False 12. True
- Kind/Nasty, Gentle/Harsh, Generous/Selfish, Loving/Hateful, Giving/Mean, Obedient/Naughty, Joyful/Grumpy, Helpful/Difficult, Respectful/Rude, Humble/Proud

New Testament Activity Answers

The Baby in the Stable (Pages 92–93)

This shepherd is wearing glasses.

- 'Glory to God in the highest heaven, and peace on earth to those with whom he is pleased!' (Luke 2 v 14)

The Boy Who Wasn't Lost (Pages 98–99)

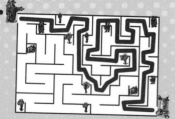

The First Followers (Pages 104–105)

- Sarah caught the biggest fish and Benny caught the smallest fish.
- When we <u>follow</u> Jesus, He can be our <u>Friend</u> and <u>walk</u> beside us every day. He <u>forgives</u> us when we tell Him we're <u>sorry</u> for the things we do <u>wrong</u>. Then we can <u>live</u> <u>lives</u> that make God <u>happy</u>, and one day we will be with Him <u>forever</u>.

Just Like Mary (Pages 110–111)

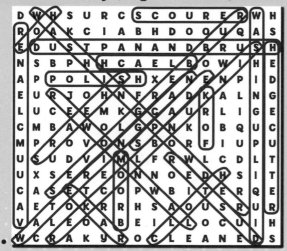

• 1. True 2. False 3. False 4. False 5. True
6. True 7. True 8. False 9. True 10. False
11. True 12. False

God's Love (Pages 116–117)

• 1. Crowds of people 2. Ill, sad, lonely and
worried people 3. So that people could see
and hear Him and He could see them more
easily, too 4. Number one 5. Moths and rust
6. Heaven 7. God and money 8. Food to
eat, proper clothes 9. Birds 10. Solomon's
11. Loves, need 12. Tomorrow

• 'I pray that Christ will make his home in
your hearts through faith. I pray that you
may have your roots and foundation in
love, so that you, together with all God's
people, may have the power to understand
how broad and long, how high and deep, is
Christ's love.' (Ephesians 3 v 17–18)

The Seed Story (Pages 122–123)

• 1. Rose 2. Hyacinth 3. Pansy 4. Tulip
5. Primrose 6. Buttercup 7. Snapdragon
8. Daffodil 9. Daisy 10. Cornflower
11. Narcissus 12. Geranium

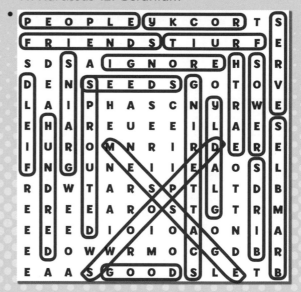

The One Who Came Back
(Pages 128–129)

This man has shorter hair than the others.

The Water-Walker (Pages 134–135)

- 1. He walked for miles, helping and teaching people 2. Having time on His own with God 3. Get into the boat and go on ahead to the other side of the lake 4. Up a hill 5. Windy 6. He walked on the water 7. A ghost 8. Peter 9. He took his eyes off Jesus 10. He reached out and grabbed hold of him 11. The weather calmed down 12. The Son of God

- 'The Lord is my helper, I will not be afraid. What can anyone do to me?' (Hebrews 13 v 6)

Alive and Well! (Pages 140–141)

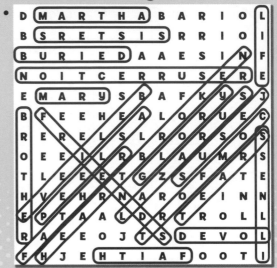

- 1. False 2. False 3. True 4. False 5. False 6. True 7. True 8. False 9. True 10. True 11. False 12. True

The Fantastic Party (Pages 146–147)

- 1. Lemonade 2. Crisps 3. Balloons 4. Sausages on sticks 5. Ice cream 6. Party poppers 7. Cheesy biscuits 8. Grapes 9. Games 10. Fairy cakes 11. Music 12. Jam sandwiches

- 'Listen! I stand at the door and knock; if anyone hears my voice and opens the door, I will come in and eat with them, and they will eat with me.' (Revelation 3 v 20)

Jesus in Jerusalem (Pages 152–153)

- 'Shout for joy, you people of Jerusalem! Look, your king is coming to you! He comes triumphant and victorious, but humble and riding on a donkey' (Zechariah 9 v 9)

-

  'I am the way, the truth, and the life; no one goes to the Father except by me.'

God's Great Plan (Pages 158–159)

- 'For God loved the world so much that he gave his only Son, so that everyone who believes in him may not die but have eternal life.' (John 3 v 16)

-

Out of the Tomb! (Pages 164–165)

-

- 1. On the first Sunday morning after Jesus died 2. An earthquake 3. An angel of the Lord 4. The stone 5. They fainted 6. He had been raised 7. 'Peace be with you' 8. They fell onto their knees and worshipped Him 9. 'Go and tell my brothers to go to Galilee, and there they will see me' 10. On a hill 11. Go to people everywhere and make them Jesus' disciples 12. Always, to the end of the age

Jesus' Promise (Pages 170–171)

- 1. True 2. True 3. False 4. True 5. True 6. False 7. False 8. False 9. True 10. False 11. True 12. False

- With Jesus BESIDE us and the Holy Spirit INSIDE us, we're never on our own. We're a part of God's family forever and ever!

BIBLE READING NOTES

Topz is a popular bimonthly devotional for 7- to 11-year-olds. The Topz Gang teach biblical truths through daily Bible readings, word games, puzzles, riddles, cartoons, competitions and simple prayers. Available as an annual subscription (6 bimonthly issues) or as single issues.

TOPZ SECRET STORIES

The *Topz Secret Stories* are full of fun as they help readers discover things about themselves and God. They include relevant biblical insight as the rival Dixons Gang cause problems and opportunities for the Topz Gang.

TOPZ SECRET DIARIES

Take a sneak peek into the lives of each member of Topz in their *Topz Secret Diaries*. Bursting with diary entries, puzzles and things to do, this series helps readers find out more about God and their relationship with Him.

TOPZ GOSPELS

Join the whole Topz Gang on more fun adventures as they explore each Gospel as children living in Bible times.

For current prices and the full *Topz* range, visit **www.cwr.org.uk/topz**